Poems from Pandemia

Poems from Pandemia

editor: Patrick Cotter

SOUTHWORD*editions*

First published in 2020
by Southword Editions
The Munster Literature Centre
Frank O'Connor House, 84 Douglas Street
Cork, Ireland
www.munsterlit.ie

Set in Centaur

ISBN 978-1-905002-82-5

The Munster Literature Centre is grateful for support from

Contents

The Dead and the Dying

The New Normal

Hope/Between Waves

Preface

In a world before antibiotics and a whole armoury of vaccines existed, my grandmother lost two infant daughters to whooping cough and a husband to tuberculosis. Her lifelong grief showed itself partly in an attachment to carbolic soap – ordinary soap was never good enough to protect a family. The nostril-grating scent of a coal-tar-derived red substance is integral to my memory of her, whose demonstrations of love included never letting me eat an apple without peeling the skin, who insisted on all raw food being scrubbed clean before being eaten. She taught me as a toddler I should never drink from anyone else's glass or take food from even a relative's fork.

She had learnt the hard way the malevolent power of microbes and their tendency to rely on thoughtless trust to spread and multiply. Growing up with an armful of vaccinations and a well-stocked chemist shop on every street corner I learnt to forget those lessons.

But the loss of children, the subsequent despair, is a Jungian heirloom one cannot renounce, even when never talked about. As Larkin might have put it, it runs from generation to generation deeper than a continental shelf. Lessons learnt the hard way, in days without effective vaccines and curative care, will eventually re-emerge with the subsurface power of glaciers.

In recent times her lessons and admonitions have recrowded my head. Nowadays in markets I walk past the displays of uncovered fruit and vegetables, the piles of mushrooms and carrots and pears which strangers can handle or cough all over before I come along. I marvel at the risks taken by shoppers who have no understanding of, no belonging to, a family bereaved by infants killed by infection, no understanding, yet – so that they casually, even now, as the year 2020 nears its end, pick up a peach to give it a squeeze, before putting it back down and pick up another to place in their basket. The new normal is shaping up to be only the older normal our ancestors lived with.

This anthology owes its origins to the cancelled 2020 Cork International Poetry Festival scheduled to take place March 24th to 28th.

Things started looking dire in Europe when hospitals in Northern Italy began to fill up in February. In early March people in Dublin were dumbfounded when scores of Italian fans were allowed to fly in for a pair of rugby matches which had been cancelled. The following week a major super-spreader event occurred when British authorities refused to cancel Cheltenham race meet and thousands of Irish fans ignored public health advice not to travel over. Around this time an Irish nursing home was reprimanded by the authorities for going into premature lockdown and Irish institutions in general were instructed not to take unilateral action relating to the crisis, as 'the virus spread in the community was low'.

We now know this 'scientific fact' was wrong, the virus was raging, undertested and under-detected. The particular scientists in charge, at this early stage, showed little awareness of the concept of exponential growth and the need for prevention of outbreaks rather than their mere management.

American poets began cancelling their festival participation under instruction from their universities. I grew more agitated as days went by and conditions seemed to be changing at breakneck speed. With the Irish authorities' admonition not to take unilateral action ringing in my ears, I continued with preparations for the festival with dreaded visualisations of a last minute cancelling, too late to stop European and British poets landing in Cork. By March 12th I was writing to the Irish Arts Council seeking permission to cancel the festival, 80% of our funding comes from government sources. The following morning I received a response instructing me I could cancel the festival if I felt it was not safe to continue. Four hours later the government announced the cancellation of the annual St Patrick's Day festival after weeks of growing feverish pressure from public opinion. I went home with a viral infection and took to my bed for two weeks, spending more weeks recovering, suffering the longest illness I had suffered since 1969 when I had succumbed to the Hong Kong flu. Nursing homes in Ireland were not issued with pandemic guidance by government officials until March 21st. The country went into full lockdown on March 27th.

In early April I decided to spend what was left of the festival budget on emergency covid bursaries for local writers and on fees for this anthology. I invited poets who had been due to appear at the festival to submit a poem. I expanded the list with some other poets who had developed a relationship with the festival over the years. I wanted to give people the widest scope while staying on topic. I wrote "We are looking for poems of hope or its lack which are about Corvid 19 or an historical/ fantasy plague; poems which are autobiographical/confessional or surreal/allegorical."

Later I allowed presubscribers to the anthology a chance to submit poems and the result is the book you are holding in your hands – which goes to press at the beginning of November, just as Europe is experiencing a second wave shaping up to be worse than the first. With its accounts of life changed utterly, lives abruptly finished, testimonies of the poignancy, the loneliness and sometimes madness of lockdown, this book is an essential statement of record on the dark times we are living through. The chapter on hope in this book is short – but this is a story set to continue for a while, many more poems will be written about it, even hopeful ones I expect, which is why I have allowed blank pages towards the end of the book for you to paste in other poems, even poems not yet written, about these dark times, even poems you may write yourself.

Patrick Cotter
Cork
October 28th 2020

Banes of Yore

James Harpur

Magna Karistia

'I leave parchment to continue this work, if perchance any man survive and any of the race of Adam escape this pestilence and carry on the work which I have begun.'
FRIAR JOHN CLYN, KILKENNY, 1349

Lord, your work is now reversed.
No cockcrows spit the bloody dawn
Wheat whispers like fields of glittering wasps
The fruits of orchards hang down
Fat and untested...we crumble to the dust
From which we were once born.

How can all this dying bring redemption?
How will you burn us into angels
With skin of gold of the light of sun
From blackened bodies dumped in wells?
Forgive my doubts of heaven
Amid the sweet miasma of this hell.

Who will survive to shoot memories
From age to age like swallows
Joining distant countries?
Who will preserve fire, earth, snow
The first green shivering of trees
The flow of pilgrims to the Barrow?

The reason that you made us –
Surely – was to witness your creation?
Without us what will be your purpose
As you walk around your garden
In eardrum-silence, echoes
Of the hooves of Death spreading on

And on – each night my sleep is beating
Over what my being has amounted to
Beyond cold vigils, chanting
The isolation of beatitude
Always giving thanks and never doubting
Why so much of it was due.

I gave my youth to find your paradise
Within this cell and cloister
Now every little sacrifice
Flares and rages – has stripped me to a pair
Of jittery fiery eyes
Skidding off corpses everywhere.

Lord, for years I have been dying
Leeched white by sterile days,
Lacklustre nights; instead of trying
To exorcise the haze
Of tepid piety – instead of crying
Out for grace, I mouthed your praise

While desperate to feel your fire in me,
Yet dreaded it, resisted till the kiss
Of apathy
Or warm embrace of fickleness
Would welcome my return to the
Familiar chapel of my emptiness.

You could have driven me pure
Transfigured me with light – one vision
Just one! would have made me sure
This life of yours was really mine.
Each day, like a dog, I waited for
Your unmistakeable sign

And now it comes – as flaming blood
Distilling fear to keener fear
And no escape; no ark bobs on the flood
Of this fetid waveless atmosphere –
The dark age has come – God
Deliver me, prepare

My soul...the world's light darkens,
The future tunnels to the past.
This blank paper is my afterlife, a token
Of the hope I've lost.
Lord start again. Make the earth
Afresh from this

Great Dearth

Mara Adamitz Scrupe

LITTLE ICE AGE

come come   *come*
tearing in little ice age/ short sprouting seasons & four centuries' failing crops
signify nothing to you now ordering your groceries online/ sheltering safe but homely

in our span in *aenigmate*
in apocalypse of flood & famine & contagion & cannibalism & infanticide & before
the dawn we looked through that glass darkly/ searching/ dissimulating

& in impromptu burlesque
in the time it takes to say a miserere/ we applied for absolution for our trespasses/ sought
inward the causal breach/ the stone seat/ our wastes washed & flowed away the stench

in streams of sin so ripe
of rotted meat   *O wash me more & more from my guilt & cleanse me from my*
sin O purify me then I shall be clean   crushed alike – the weak & strong – & angels

in different colors – of silver &
gold –
we asked for their forgiveness/ offered stamped coin & umbrage & glittering curses/ lusts
& loves of ancient cavaliers grudges of gladiators & bull terriers' gripped digits

in graverobbers' haul – finger
bones of copper bronzed poetry – matrices of blue-bruised & furtive/ ossein & proximal
we perished of other plagues our posy rings bespoke: *I give it thee to think*   *on mee*

Cheryll Pearson

Plague Village, Eyam

In the church, the windows sing. One priest
in lush colour, a dead faint. Two jewelled lovers

split by a river. *They tucked their grandmothers*
under the roses. Their sons under heather.

The secrets those chocolate-box cottages harbour
under gnomes and magnolia. *If the horse had spooked*

and bucked its load — If the bolt of silk had been dry —
They must have lived on knees for weeks, all praise

and bruising. Their old trespasses troubled the milk.
Raised the occasional hive. What sin could have hollowed

the cottages? *If the city had sounded the bell — If*
the fleas hadn't roused — Years of moons and christenings.

Loaves and vows. Elsewhere they glove new lambs
into barns. Make and marry with cool brows.

Thomas McCarthy

A Medical History of County Cork

That our first Professor of Medicine was the son
Of a Macroom noblewoman who lamented her Austrian Hussar

Was of little consequence when the first newly-qualified
House Officer died. You,

Go tell his mother —

The anxious mother of the young rider
Whose horse came home rider-less from Skibbereen.

You, go tell her what a pandemic fever has done.
The parchment was hardly dry on his degree.

Such news always has to come home and settle in a mother:
Only afterwards is it history,

As now when the bad news of people falling away from life
First reaches Bandon, then the city,

Then the County clerk who will fill in the blank spaces
In the weekly return of the lost.

Afterwards, they will all marvel at the sheer number
Of the dead. Yet it was all over,

In the deepest possible sense, when the first mother in Cork
Fell to her knees, seeking one word from God.

Alan Shapiro

Extract from PASSAGE OUT

JUNE 20

Ship fever, faster than a fire,
has broken out. And over fifty
of the hundred shut up in the dark,
unventilated hold are dying.
The "Mistress," as my wife is called,
tends whom she can but can do little
more than to ease their agony,
she quiets it, with laudanum.
Still, "Mistress, please, for God's sake, water"
rises with the effluvium,
the shroud of stench that can be seen,
but not breathed, covering the deck.

JUNE 23

A deputation came on deck,
fifteen or more, demanding water
for their sick ones below. Said they
would rush the store and help themselves;
"Are we to drink the diarrhoea?"
As helpless as they were enraged,
most could not even make a fist
or raise their arms.
                              One cruel mate seeing
but a relief from tedium
laughed at their threats and, for form's sake,
fired his gun into the air.
And the great bang hit them like a shot.
Some fell down to their knees, and begged;
the rest turned, climbing through the hatch
meekly, to face their families.

JUNE 27

The dead are going overboard
without prayer, and with little sorrow
(for few have life enough for grief).
Like spoiled meat, husbands, wives, and children
thrown overboard into the deep-
as if this were their last kind act
that now they can relieve their kin
who have at last when they lie down
some room to change position in.

JULY 9

At noon a brig about two miles
off starboard bow came into view.
And I am sure we looked to them
as they to us: serene against
the glister of the soft, green waves,
sunlight glinting off the bow,
the sails like blossoms on the wind
full as the white clouds, and as new.

JULY 30
Gross Isle, Canada

The foul mattresses, huge barrels
of vilest matter, the rags and clothes
dumped from the ships that came before us,
dumped in this river that is now
undrinkable, this water we
for weeks have dreamed of.
                              When we anchored
the doctor came on board and said,
"Ha, there is fever here," and left.
And since then, now almost a week,
only the dead are brought to shore.
The rest must wait till there is room
for quarantine.
                    So from the brig
we watch while large and graceful ships

from Germany glide past with ease
bearing the robust passengers
on to their precious days. Cruel
the way they sing, the girls who laugh-
their blond hair shining in the sun-
laughing as they blow kisses to
these blighted shades who stagger out
of the dark hold, pained by the light.

AUGUST 10

After the digging, Sean McGuire,
his skin too papery to sweat,
drove two shovels into the ground
making a cross, and said, "By this,
Mary. I swear I will go back
as soon as I earn passage home
and murder him that murdered you,
our landlord, Palmerston."
                          And went,
like all the rest, like living refuse
half naked, maimed, to Montreal,
to Boston, to New York; the seeds
of typhus already blossoming.

And blossoming those other seeds
as virulent as a disease,
that grief which suffering can't feel,
that will return as surely as
the seasons when the flesh returns.
Who have endured must now endure
a healing no less unbearable,
must be consoled by hate's cold feel
fixing all their memories
into a purpose stronger than life,
immutable as loss.
                        They go,
and may God go with them who bring
into the new world nothing else
but epitaphs for legacies.

Tony Curtis

Claude and Chouchou at Le Moulleau, 1916

It is cool beneath the pines where they sit
after their hard climb over the Dune du Pilat
with their picnic under its cloth in the basket.
A father and daughter in the sea breeze
and shadows - *En blanc et noir.*

He still wears a striped, light summer suit,
bow tie and a straw boater, but his eyes
are furrowed behind his wire-framed glasses.
Chouchou in a white, loose dress and her large, floppy hat
with the white flower appliquéd; her holiday shoes
from which she has shaken the sand.

The sound of the sea-shore soothes -
they are two years into a war that may never end;
he has cancer and she will die of diphtheria within a year.
But for this afternoon the sun swims through the trees;
she will close her eyes and hear the Atlantic playing its etudes
and her father's *La Mer.*

They are miles further south from *la cathédrale engloutie,*
the rough coast and myths of Brittany.
High above this town is Notre-Dame des Passes;
they have climbed all those church steps and looked across
at Cap Ferret's lighthouse, its red dome bright
against the two clear blues of sky and sea.

Everything will be precious from this day,
these hours taken from painful times.
As Emma's camera fixes their lives in this moment
their dog has heard something in the pines
and turns its head to look away.

Martín Espada

The Five Horses of Doctor Ramón Emeterio Betances
Mayagüez, Puerto Rico 1856

I. The First Horse
Cholera swarmed unseen through the water, lurking in wells and fountains,
squirming in garbage and excrement, infinitesimal worms drilling the intestines,
till all the water and salt would pour from the body, till the body became a worm,
shriveling and writhing, a slug in salt, till the skin burned blue as flame, the skin
of the peasant and the skin of the slave gone blue, the skin in the slave barracks blue,
the skin of ten thousand slaves blue. The Blue Death, face hidden in a bandanna,
dug graves with the gravediggers, who fell into holes they shoveled for the dead.
The doctors died too, seeing the signs in the mirror, the hand with the razor shaking.

II. The Second Horse
Doctor Betances stepped off the boat, back from Paris, the humidity of the plague
glistening in his beard. He saw the stepmother who fed him sink into a mound
of dirt, her body empty as the husk of a locust in drought. He toweled off his hands.
In the quarantine tents there was laudanum by the bitter spoonful, the lemonade
and broth; in the dim of the kerosene lamps there was the compress cool against
the forehead, the elixir of the bark from the cinchona tree. For peasants and slaves moan-
ing to their gods, the doctor prescribed chilled champagne to soothe the belly.
For the commander of the Spanish garrison, there was silence bitter as the spoon.

III. The Third Horse
At every hacienda, at every plantation, as the bodies of slaves rolled one by one
into ditches all hipbones and ribs, drained of water and salt, stripped of names,
Doctor Betances commanded the torch for the barracks where the bodies would
tangle together, stacked up as if they never left the ship that sailed from Africa,
kept awake by the ravenous worms of the plague feasting upon them. Watching
the blue flames blacken the wood, the doctor and the slaves saw another plague burning
away, the plague of manacles scraping the skin from hands that cut
the cane, the plague of the collar with four spikes for the runaways brought back.

IV. The Fourth Horse

The pestilence of the masters, stirred by spoons into the coffee of the world,
spread first at the marketplace, at auction, the coins passing from hand to hand.
So Doctor Betances began, at church, with twenty-five pesos in pieces of eight,
pirate coins dropped into the hands of slaves to drop into the hands of masters, buying
their own infants at the baptismal font. The secret society of abolitionists
shoved rowboats full of runaways off the docks in the bluest hour of the blue night,
off to islands without masters. Even the doctor would strangle in the executioner's
garrote, spittle in his beard, if the soldiers on watch woke up from the opiate of empire.

V. The Fifth Horse

The governor circled his name in the name of empire, so Dr. Betances
sailed to exile, the island drowning in his sight, but a vision stung
his eyes like salt in the wind: in the world after the plague, no more
plague of manacles; after the pestilence, no more pestilence of masters;
after the cemeteries of cholera, no more collar of spikes or executioners.
In his eye burned the blue of the rebel flag and the rising of his island.
The legend calls him the doctor who exhausted five horses, sleepless
as he chased invisible armies into the night. Listen for the horses.

John Fitzgerald

RESISTANCE

We're safe enough,
I whispered to myself
and the turkey hanging
from the curtain rail.

We dry between our toes
won't eat orange ice-lolls
air our clothes.
And we have Granny

on our side. Nothing
would get past Nora
Twomey at our back
door (the front was

sealed up for good).
Nora, who wrote
cheques aged fourteen
and managed her father's

counters while he
hankered for the farm
she gave him when
she married Dan Fitz.

You could see it written
in the lines across her face
until the day she died:
NO POLIO HERE.

Eiléan Ní Chuilleanáin

THE POLIO EPIDEMIC

No hurry at all in house or garden,
The children were kept from the danger --
The parents suddenly had more time
To watch them, to keep them amused,
To see they had plenty to read.
The city lay empty, infected.
There was no more ice-cream.
The baths were closed all summer.

One day my father allowed me beyond the gate
With a message to pass through a slit in a blank wall;
I promised I would just cycle for two hours,
Not stop or talk, and I roamed the long roads
Clear through city and suburbs, past new churches,
Past ridges of houses where strange children
Were kept indoors too, I sliced through miles of air,
Free as a plague angel descending
On places the buses went: Commons Road, Friars' Walk.

Martín Espada

LETTER TO MY FATHER
October 2017

You once said: *My reward for this life will be a thousand pounds of dirt*
shoveled in my face. You were wrong. You are seven pounds of ashes
in a box, a Puerto Rican flag wrapped around you, next to a red brick
from the house in Utuado where you were born, all crammed together
on my bookshelf. You taught me there is no God, no life after this life,
so I know you are not watching me type this letter over my shoulder.

When I was a boy, you were God. I watched from the seventh floor
of the projects as you walked down into the street to stop a public
execution. A big man caught a small man stealing his car, and everyone
in Brooklyn heard the car alarm wail of the condemned: *He's killing me.*
At a word from you, the executioner's hand slipped from the hair
of the thief. *The kid was high,* was all you said when you came back to us.

When I was a boy, and you were God, we flew to Puerto Rico. You said:
My grandfather was the mayor of Utuado. His name was Buenaventura.
That means good fortune. I believed in your grandfather's name.
I heard the tree frogs chanting to each other all night. I saw banana
leaf and elephant palm sprouting from the mountain's belly. I gnawed
the mango's pit, and the sweet yellow hair stuck between my teeth.
I said to you: *You came from another planet. How did you do it?*
You said: *Every morning, just before I woke up, I saw the mountains.*

Every morning, I see the mountains. In Utuado, three sisters,
all in their seventies, all bedridden, all Pentecostales who only left
the house for church, lay sleeping on mattresses spread across the floor
when the hurricane gutted the mountain the way a butcher slices open
a dangled pig, and a rolling wall of mud buried them, leaving the fourth
sister to stagger into the street, screaming like an unheeded prophet
about the end of the world. In Utuado, a man who cultivated a garden
of aguacate and carambola, feeding the avocado and star fruit to his
nieces from New York, saw the trees in his garden beheaded all at once
like the soldiers of a beaten army, and so hanged himself. In Utuado,
a welder and a handyman rigged a pulley with a shopping cart to ferry

rice and beans across the river where the bridge collapsed, witnessed
the cart swaying above so many hands, then raised a sign that told
the helicopters: *Campamento los Olvidados: Camp of the Forgotten.*

Los olvidados wait seven hours in line for a government meal of Skittles
and Vienna sausage, or a tarp to cover the bones of a house with no roof,
as the fungus grows on their skin from sleeping on mattresses drenched
with the spit of the hurricane. They drink the brown water, waiting
for microscopic monsters in their bellies to visit plagues upon them.
A nurse says: These people are going to have an epidemic. *These people
are going to die.* The president flips rolls of paper towels to a crowd
at a church in Guaynabo, Zeus lobbing thunderbolts on the locked ward
of his delusions. Down the block, cousin Ricardo, Bernice's boy, says
that somebody stole his can of diesel. I heard somebody ask you once
what Puerto Rico needed to be free. And you said: *Tres pulgadas
de sangre en la calle: Three inches of blood in the street.* Now, three
inches of mud flow through the streets of Utuado, and troops patrol
the town, as if guarding the vein of copper in the ground, as if a shovel
digging graves in the back yard might strike the ore below, as if la brigada
swinging machetes to clear the road might remember the last uprising.

I know you are not God. I have the proof: seven pounds of ashes in a box
on my bookshelf. Gods do not die, and yet I want you to be God again.
Stride from the crowd to seize the president's arm before another roll
of paper towels sails away. Thunder Spanish obscenities in his face.
Banish him to a roofless rainstorm in Utuado, so he unravels, one soaked
sheet after another, till there is nothing left but his cardboard heart.

I promised myself I would stop talking to you, white box of grey grit.
You were deaf even before you died. Hear my promise now: I will take you
to the mountains, where houses lost like ships at sea rise blue and yellow
from the mud. I will open my hands. I will scatter your ashes in Utuado.

Jon McLeod

A Sagitation

On days like these I think of Saint Sebastian
against an arch on the palace steps,
pierced with two hundred arrowheads,

as Emperor Diocletian, who assumed
the job was properly done, halts
his coach briefly to hear him rattle on,

then commands a second round,
cudgel blows beyond the city walls,
body dumped down an open drain.

When the plagues came, the city folk
would say the crusted pustules
were apertures to sweet Sebastian's

untainted skin, *don't give in,* they'd say
pray, do what you must to live again.

Imaginary Pestilences

John Mee

ZOONOSES

are what we catch
from animals, even our pets,

when we lean
too close, breathe in

what they breathe out.
Our noses twitch-

too long chained down,
they get the itch

to swap places
with a proboscis,

trunk or snout.
Before my wife can shout

Leave the cat alone, for Christ's sake,
Pooka has my rhinitis

and I'm smelling
the world in HD,

head exploding
with grassy memory,

new tail swishing.
As Pooka powers up

my laptop
to check the Guardian,

I'm out in the garden
pissing on a tree.

Rebecca Tamás

The Future

I walked under glass domes, the sunshine was perpetual,
the smell of plant life intense, overwhelming.

I had thought this would be my chance to move to another world
before it was too late, a chance to set myself up for life,
to escape the fumes and the sickness,
embrace sunsets in ice cream colours,
eight suns rising in the sky, like a tarantula's eyes.

If I describe the intensely unpleasant joy
of seeing a lover that spurned you in the street,
making mute small talk with them, yawning,
do you know what I'm talking about?
The way that your inside regions are burning,
your stomach is fizzing with acid, your are eyes pricking
with vinegar sharpness – but outside, nothing.
No blush mounting, no downward
turn of the mouth. To play the part so well it hurts him!
So well it makes him wonder if you even cared at all.

Then to half wave and walk and away,
pretending to check your phone,
remembering how he kissed you in the deli and
made your skin collapse.
Remembering being crushed into a cupboard at
a party and saying, 'I'm attracted to you on a cellular level,'
his green eyes going wide and uncertain, creeped
out at the stink of perfume on your breath.
The whole outline of his body is rising like a disgusting bruise
inside your own, and not a flicker,
not a single bead of sweat as you leave him,
though his face opens again and again on the sheet of your mind,
an unfurling bloom.

That is the overwhelming sense of my new habitat,
missing the old home so much I get sick,
but knowing I can never return.
Knowing that this punishment is what I waited for,
head under the covers, wondering how many pieces one body
can be split into before it entirely falls apart.

This place was never meant for me, rejects me like a donor heart,
but I won't leave – disgusting limpet of a failed design.
One day here is shorter than a year, and the atmosphere
is turning my sockets silver, my hands becoming frail and feathery as wings.

No one can imagine the perverted, lustrous, terrible life we are growing here,
hot blue grass rising up like serpent's teeth.

Cory Ingram

Voices Of Galata

I

Ishak

selam!

he sweeps the leaves from the stoop
the March light flooding the
ides of sleepless nights

will you close?

essential service! coffee?
the clink of porcelain
a smiling moon in an ochre scarf

here—sit—drink
go back to Galata
sun on your face

you remember that day?

yes you smelling of hammam as I
shaved the week from your neck
white fists on the chair
trust I've felt much life under this blade
comes and goes but always the
green leaf follows the cold wind

Azra

typo
closed but maybe not so temporary
rain whips through the sweeping door
smell of dust to dust

he says not to worry
waning moon is still bright

the köfte will not cook itself she says
Ramadan without loved ones is not Ramadan
funerals are not funerals

she stands at the window
a brave vine from the drainpipe
crawls toward the ladder
a puddle of clouds on the roof

2

Elif

mass graves will come here too
barges on the river
firebombs blessing the bodies

yeter!
you want to die? keep talking!
the rules! no one outside this house!
a crescent moon hangs!

she will not make a ritual of her hands
a sanitised prayer
she will not die of a stolen kiss

clouds come gauzily
a curl of smoke
from the lips of the boy who shows
no symptoms

Andrew

puff to puff
a mouth of peaches

her scarab eyes
like buttons of Priam's Treasure
who leaves a find like that
because of a plague?

he unlocks her lips and
tastes the myths inside
the roses of Troy
a selfie for the boys

she's burning into a fever dream
I've been here before
listen the sirens are on their way

they swing their legs over the Thames
count the bells toll
we are the moonlight
we are not yet the ashes

Hello, My Name Is Covid

Tom French

To Distance

the withering god of fever swoops on us
Sophocles, *Oedipus Rex*

Si les temps sont durs et mauvais, pour qui le sont-ils?
Homemade Netflix

It is being
snowbound without snow,
able to move with nowhere to go.

The churches are closed,
Masses are streamed.
The Sign of Peace is suspended,
the holy water fonts are drained.

Outside St Peter's the man I meet,
teetering on the verge of tears,
shows me the breach he's made
in the crowd control barriers.

'Mind yourself', I go
and find I mean it.

*

When we could look up from the shore
the candles lit for good intentions
were a string of tiny lighthouses.

*

We take *Steriwipes* to telephones
and join, in a gesture of prayer,
our hands before our breastbones.

*

There's a virtual queue
for the only copy the county owns
of Defoe's *A Journal of the Plague Year*
that hasn't been out of the store in years,

and will have to be quarantined
for seventy-two hours when it returns.

*

All of the shelves in our new Aldi
that stands where the nursing home
used to stand, are empty.

                A shopper,
trying to decide between two last things,
gives up and decides she doesn't need either.

*

I remember a day ago like it was ....
We think twice before touching a thing
and begin to long for the touch of a hand.

My own are so clean I feel
I am being prepared for a surgery
I did not even know I need.

*

I do what I have never done —

remove my wedding ring
because it 'harbours infection',
and find, printed on the skin
beneath, its pale reflection.

*

A Japanese aquarium wants people
to video call their eels
'so the creatures will remember
that humans exist
and not become a threat.'

I dial, and wait, then put the phone away
not just because of dread
of their voice mail kicking in
but because it dawns on me,
beyond the ordinary niceties,

I wouldn't know what to say.

I top up the mower
and wait for the grass to grow
so I can cut it again.

*

A stone's throw from the sea,
I shell out for a Penguin *Selected Hardy*
with the exact coins to avoid contact
in the charity shop the last day it opens,

and read the *Veteris Vestigia Flammae poems* —
            Why do you make me leave the house
            and think for a breath it is you I see —
wearing a pair of blue disposable gloves.

*

All the meetings that were really emails,
the emails that might have been phone calls,
come back to haunt us in the small hours.

'I am not here'. .. 'I will reply . . .'
'I am not on leave' . . . I leave
an out-of-office to account for me

and queue in the carpark for saplings
which I place on the passenger seat
with their roots in the footwell
and, with the sun behind me, drive east.

They are my passengers.
This will be their ultimate journey.

*

I takes me an age to realise
what I'm watching is not a GIF —
the fox some wannabe shopper shot
with an *iPhone* on Grafton Street.

It keeps The Traitor's Arch behind it,
passes McDaid's and Neary's
like they weren't there, and hangs
the left that leads to the door of Grogan's.

*

We stay away to give the elders,
extending their arms behind glass
in gestures of embrace, a chance.

When the worst is over —
(I almost wrote 'the world') —
we will remind them who we are,
that we never stopped loving them
even if why we kept away eludes them.

*

Silver and Common and Downy Birch,
Rowan, Wild Cherry, Field Maple,
Crab Apple, Alder, Holly, Oak.
Saying the names does a power of good.

While we waited for the all clear
we'll be able to say we planted trees.

*

It will be years before they touch;
still, we plant them ten feet apart.

*

The coining of a new verb — 'to cocoon' —
to care for whilst never being in the same room —
sends me to check what I think it means
and from where it is I think it comes.

The Occitan *coco* and the French *cocon*
remind me of what I never knew
as each emerges from the previous one.

*

Neighbours salute their neighbour's body
the way they would if they passed him
heading into the village for messages,
on the two mile drive to the cemetery.

*

All I get, when I check for an update just now —
'Everything's safe and sound in *Samsung Cloud*'.

*

Since the body is almost all water
it is natural that whole swathes of time
should disappear in watching
a jellyfish swim in St Mark's Square.

It is a glimpse of the world without us,
a glimpse of how it used to and will be —
canal water clearer than anyone
can remember, and *Rhizostoma pulmo*

moving like a silk gown through air,
catching the currents so gracefully
it barely disturbs its reflection
passing through the empty streets.

*

In the annals of bidding goodnight
it passes for a kind of milestone
when my youngest presents
her elbow for the first time,
and I answer hers with mine.

This is the wink and elbow language of goodnight.

*

There isn't a fridge freezer
to be bought for twenty miles
within twenty-four hours.

*

The pubs are closed ... all of them.
Now we are officially 'the worried well'
who wake from dreams of being
parched and raising drinks to our lips,
to somebody calling 'Time'.

*

Out of nowhere
the *Rescue* helicopter;

then, as if it has released
them above us, a flight of geese.

*

At the checkpoint on the coast road
the last time it was – 'Where are you
coming from?' and 'Where are you going?',
'Have you any idea what speed you were doing?'

Now, when I slow on my bike to account
for myself – 'I'm going home' – to the woman
in uniform at the checkpoint, she laughs
and steps into the verge and waves me on.

*

We hear the Taoiseach say
'The next ten days will be crucial',
and read in the broadsheet the man in West Clare –
'I have been social isolating for the last ten years.'

*

In the last storm it was bread.
This time it is flour.
Though we don't know how
to pronounce it, we learn
to recognise the Polish for 'yeast'.

The next time we will fight
each other in the fields for wheat.

Terror of having nothing to read
makes me confirm my humanity
by turning, with one click,
an 'I am not a robot' box
into a green tick.

The birthday party from which no-one goes home
is the one my friend attends with his friends by *Zoom*.

Though they go all out and get dressed up
the empties they wake to are theirs alone.

The only certainty is where they've been.

The cortege hardly warrants the name.
We form a guard of honour at our gates
and catch the rest inside on Funerals Live,
the oxymoron we might have been spared.

The service is broadcast quality.
You'd be hard pressed to tell
camera man from undertaker's man.

He saves to an external drive,
handles his tripod deftly like a bier,
converts the service to a compact format
and knows how much bandwidth grief needs.

A measure of the gravity of the situation –
adolescents remove headphones to listen
to the Taoiseach's 9pm address to the nation.

Like a weatherman paraphrasing Churchill
he speaks of the storm that is yet to come
as the medics in the Far East head home.

How true Jones's *Treatise on Skating* reads
as a sick world posts selfies with a super moon
and a cortege of red *Transit* vans draws up
at the ice rink requisitioned to act as a mortuary —

The arms will be held out in front at first
and permitted later to cross at the breast.

All of the skates are in their cubicles.
The stretcher bearers put on ice shoes.
A mortician takes a reading
and lowers the thermostat a degree.

✻

The car plant stops making cars
and modifies windscreen wiper motors,
the sensors intended to detect rain,
to manufacture ventilators.

✻

Overnight,
simply by printing new labels,
the distillers of gin
become hand sanitiser makers.

Now every hour is cocktail hour.
By the bathroom sink — tonic, lemon.
This bar is called *The Smallest Room.*

I am one of its handful of regulars
who have no home to go to but this,
whose hands will never be this clean again.

✻

Good Friday.
Christ, it is 'unseasonably warm'.
At three o'clock in the afternoon
I read that skiing goggles have appeared in ICUs,

that the front line print off headshots
and *Sellotape* them to their gowns,
and when gowns run out, to aprons.

✻

On a hand-held device we watch
the hand washing video
we didn't know we needed –

Gloria Gaynor rolling up her sleeves
and giving hers the treatment
to the whole of 'I Will Survive',
then rinsing and rinsing and rinsing
like you wouldn't believe.

✻

Which beats hands down
singing 'Happy Birthday' twice
twenty times a day,

or 'Baby Shark' – Christ spare me –
and only ever getting
halfway through 'Daddy ...'

✻

The doorbell ...!
Who in the name of Jesus could that be?

And when the penny drops with somebody
finally to do what you do – open the door –
who's standing there only nobody.

✻

Across the back fields
to the first deer tracks;
then, by the roads,
to the cemetery and back.

This was always the extent of my life —
never a moment
when I was not within
shouting distance of home.

*

Becoming a Christian
becomes a hit-and-miss affair —
a priest, performing a baptism,

fills a water gun with holy water
and, closing an eye to take aim,
makes a cross below the hairline
of the target held aloft by its father.

*

O, to be in Italy
where everywhere you turn
home-made signs on balconies
read 'Andrà tutto bene',

and in Assisi where,
across the deserted *piazze*,
the self-isolated sing
to keep each other company.

*

The council, without breathing
a word, stockpiles plywood
to cover spaces in the near future
where windows used to be.

It is not newsworthy.
This is the music
of what happens
behind the scenes.

*

Nobody knows the answer.
The silence in the air
after the question is posed —
'Can snow ploughs be adapted
to dig mass graves?' —

is akin to the silence
that comes off snow.

How is it that the first line
of that Thomas McCarthy poem goes —
        It is an image of irreversible loss . . .

Here is uncharted territory.
Who, now, will be able
to look at a clear road
without wondering where it goes?

✳

The biggest plane on Earth
flies all night from the east
and touches down, bearing
a cargo of one million gowns.

The worst of what they've seen
has yet to happen here.

✳

For the first time in a lifetime
today in Wuhan
there is blue sky, birdsong.

I read Po Chu-I —

        Now that I have tasted the joy of being alone
        I will never again come with a friend at my side —

and lie with my face to the east.

✳

I miss the sea
I stand outside
at night between
the trees to hear.

Beyond the far ditch
seagulls, in its wake,
give the plough away.

The last rig it ploughs
before it leaves
will be the access
it left to the second field.

When the birds leave
it will look like
it was never here.

✻

I want these days
to be over

I miss being out
wishing I'd stayed
at home.

✻

I cross the river on foot
to exchange a heartfelt greeting
with a total stranger.

✻

The *New Holland* working
the big field in front of us
is utterly oblivious.

✻

I have seen the trees coming into leaf.
The coast is as clear as it's ever been.

The gorse is in full bloom.
Everyone's at a distance.

The only thing
approaching
is the sea.

12 March 2020 –

Isolation

Paddy Bushe

THE ETYMOLOGY OF ISOLATION

No man is an Iland, intire of itself.

JOHN DONNE

I
Outside our window, above the wind-flecked
Bay between its two enclosing headlands,

A dozen gannets circle, now and then plunging
And struggling up to wheel and plunge again.

I am contemplating *isolation*, its meanings
In the here and now and then and again,

Contemplating that *isolate* shares its Latin
Island roots with *insulate*, that each one is also

A peece of the Continent, a part of the maine.
Isolation warms itself towards insulation.

II
I think of our son, whose house on the small
Peninsula across the bay I can just make out,

And who drops food and news and comfort
To our insulated door, like a boatman judging

A quick now or never surge to a storm-isolated
Island slipway, quickly heaving up supplies

One-handed, the other on the tiller steering
A curve astern. He smiles, waves. Half-joking,

Wholly grateful in this semi-isolation, I offer
A coinage: *peninsulated.* We'll live with that.

Patrick Cotter

March 2020

One for sorrow, two for joy

On Wednesday even the birds chose to self-isolate.
There was no ominous magpie in her singledom to violate
the still air across my window with her Bren gun chatter
or with her bomb-like swoop, as if made of incendiary matter.
The part of girl and part of boy, the part of silver and part of gold
did not emerge but stayed hidden like a secret too unseemly unbold
to bolt from the sweet foraged foliage of acid-blued hydrangea,
too restrained to disturb the off-to-save-the-life-of-a-stranger
Asian nurse, plodding past in black cotton cardigan
the sight of her, stopping my heart turning hard again.

Will Harris

Lockdown

so you get out and it's central
london hotter than the central
line in august if you're reading this
out loud stop it the national
gallery is shut let's just talk I'm offering
you my hand remember when
that was enough we held hands not
forever but as a theory of being which is
something   come on   I'm talking to you
not burger king though you'd say
what's the difference   everywhere's shut
or laying people off the ghouls are circling
but there used to be a bakery here
that did pork buns and we could sit outside
reading urn & drum and diane di prima
the stakes are myself she said   and now I
realise what she meant there is no
other me but me in you stop
reading

Paula Bohince

INTERIORS

When the outside emptied by decree,

when the toxic invisible took shape in pixels—
        barbed mist, a redness—

        when our very breath
was suspicious: laughter masked, singing

        a luxury of *before*.

When we became perceptive
        as put-upon animals, as in the vigilant child-

hood, those zombie'd days re-risen.

        When we escaped into the adaptation
of Romeo and Juliet,

        glassy eyes of her wanting
against his quickening *yes, yes*, and then, and then

the kiss, the memory
of it replaying in the bedded evening

as antidote to statistics.

Precious, our orbit: each other, enough flour,
a signal, a password.

We turned to the sun for medicine. We muted
        the tantrum at the podium.

        Stroking the cat, emotional against her fur,
our world was teardrop-small, reflecting

        no spring, *no, no*, no spring at all.

Enda Wyley

Through the Window
for my mother

Odd but necessary the solution that comes to us,
to stare through glass at you: your parched face
slanted towards the afternoon light. On your wall
a forest you'd painted when we were young.

Two red coated figures walk under trees
and we remember the bedtime story you read us —
wardrobe portal into snow, a lamppost, Narnia's wood.
Now, here is the masked carer, opening the window

to the love we yell in — such force it unsettles you.
We're ready to turn back to our strange world
where we stand apart, can't touch, but lucky
we've seen your lips pucker into one last kiss.

Breda Joyce

On her First Visit to my Aunt in the Nursing Home

My mother's eyes hug her sister, the distance
strange between them. Leaning in
towards one another they speak with hands
that hold hope and sadness in open palms.
My mother asks if she is settling in.
I am for now, what can I do?

Before parting, my aunt casts aside her walker,
draws nearer to my mother for a photo
that will hold this visit. Then she points
to the fish tank in the corner, said she loves
the way fish swim so close to one another.
They bring colour to her confinement.

Later, I swim out from Blackrock,
the tide slack as I move west
through failing light. My arms like dials
slice through seconds in slow definite strokes
until I reach the slipway. Beneath me
sea creatures glide beyond confinement.

Rachael Hegarty

The Second Wave

Word came in last night: Unfortunately, we have been advised
that a resident who transferred to Beaumont Hospital yesterday
has tested positive for Covid 19. I recognise this is a disappointment
as many of you were looking forward to visiting this week.
I couldn't read the rest of the email, the screen blurred with tears.
Some sound came out of me innards and cracked all over the gaff.
Me husband and kids came running, the eldest grabbed me phone
and read out loud, the youngest held me hand and my love held on
to me from behind. Family photos gawked out at the state of us.
Since then it has rained non-stop and the men have taken to the kitchen.
Himself is roasting a shoulder of lamb — long, slow hours at a low heat.
Just the way me Ma likes it. Our sons are baking for Ireland — fairy cakes, brownies and
angel buns — all their nanny's favourites. I get out and garden.
I weed and make up a posy of drenched dog roses for her care package.
I have to leave it all on the doorstep of me Ma's still-locked-down care home.

Heather Treseler

Sonnet

We wake. Sing a little song
of panic breakfast. Then check
the weather. Clear the throat and
wait for the latch of rasp or
rattle. Scan the Tuesday street,
naked of children. (A stray
woman, leashed to her beagle,
nervous for privacy or
conversation.) If we are not
at home, we might poison
the air. Yet all day, we long
for his salt smell, her clutch.
Dry secret of an ancient despair:
how we grow raw with untouch.

Jane Clark

Flowers from the Hills
For Dora

Because I can't travel the miles between us,
I'll send you flowers from the hills.

Lady's bedstraw to brighten your bedroom,
placed by your pillow, it'll scent your sleep.

Scarlet pimpernel to dispel your sadness,
it wakes early as the blackbird sings.

Crane's-bill, herb-robert, ragged robin
come pink as dawn to your window.

Eyebright will heal your tired sight,
two-lipped petals, lilac-lined.

Teasel to feed goldfinch in your garden,
orange tips will drink from the leaves.

Marsh Marigold to ward off all harm,
Stitchwort sprinkled like stars at your feet.

Jed Myers

A Rise in the Wind

Say you haven't mingled since the pub
closed, and you've chosen to put up
with the aloneness as long as it takes
for the tiny death stars to disperse;

say you cocoon in whatever is home,
let the absences spin an invisible
column of silence around you, a storm's
eye, a silo to the sky;

say it's your tower, narrow venue
for your solo show, none of it streamed
live to your loves, no bows to applause
and flowers, yours the one review;

say night by private night you dine in
on unrealized hopes, reminiscences, chips
dipped in a pico de gallo of doubt,
a few shots, a little sublingual Xanax;

say you message your best friends, even
the three who are dead, and as you await
responses, you step out into the dark,
stare up and let in the oldest sparks;

say out of that black waste above you
murmurs descend, you wouldn't say
angels or ancestors but some company
enters your head, your chest, solar plexus;

say an invisible throng fills the steep
tiers of your clavicles, ribs, hip crests,
till you're an opera house, bullring, awash
in a hubbub of the legions you've missed;

say this arrival's only a rise
in the wind, the old maple's foliage
flapping gladly along with the air's latest
surge, and alright, you're going back in;

say in your bed you sweat, your isolation
broken, like a fever, and separate
as you still are, no creature of your ilk
in sight, you can't quite say alone.

Shirin Jindani

#MakingFriends

I had no friends and so I made them out of odds and ends—
a torn sheet, last year's fraying shirt, two mismatched gloves,
all cross-stitched, stuffed with plastic wrappers, bits of string,
the viscera of unpaid bills— and bound by an invisible seam.
I sewed the torso to some cut-off jeans.

Feet were easy, heads were not, asymmetric faces watched
as buckled shoes swung on pendulum legs. Inarticulate,
inclined to rip, they held their counsel zipper-lipped
and when a button-eye rolled across the floor,
the remaining eye just watched it more.

They were happy, or at least I think they were, my patchwork tribe
about chest height. They had woollen hair (some were bald)
and broadly respected social norms. They sat at tables,
lounged on chairs, wore reading glasses to check their phones
and posted selfies when left alone.

Evenings we basked in the aquarium light of deep-sea documentaries
unaware that my cloth companions had sparked an online global trend.
The viral storm broke when a series of revenge porn pics
exposed the "extravagant genitalia" of my "hand-sewn freaks".
In a non-binary world I believe we are all biologically unique.

After *a papier-mâché* shark surfaced in the middle of the bed
I furloughed my friends. Now a hermit crab occupies the reading lamp.
Distancing in a snorkel and diving mask, I meet the raised eyebrows
of the bra-muzzled supermarket manager scanning fruit
as he weighs up my home-crocheted-Lurex-all-in-one wetsuit.

Sophie Ewh

QUARANTINE WHORE

After the curfew, the skin I wear started to sag, in all the wrong places,
everywhere; it started bagged and flimsy but became cracked plastic.

After one day, George opened a window and my takeout skin sweeped out,
cleared away: now it's clear my muscles move alone, unjustified.

I am no matter. I have no matter. I don't matter;
and, down to the atom, the muscle matter of me knows this.

After five days, I stopped the Lexapro; I pulled the stopper,
poured my realness, ashed the doctor. George forgot to remind me.

After seven days, I called my therapist; I had to ask how to ask George
for space. Not space space, just space to work and masturbate and make money.

My therapist's therapist told her that other people's emotions shouldn't control your own;
so my therapist told me to tell George that I made a schedule.

After ten days, I did nothing. My unshaven legs looked like George's; I wanted to saw them,
stripe them with razor candy cane cuts. I painted my nails so our hands were different.

But after fourteen days, I had eaten all the nail polish. I couldn't separate
my hand's thoughts from his anymore; so I said, "George, I made a schedule."

I didn't tell my therapist what I was going to do when I was alone—
I became a video call girl. The John just needed a laptop and a connection.

Facetime, Skype, Zoom: not that they called to see me. I wasn't selling the body
I never had, just my voice. "I don't love you," I said, "but I know you. I will become you."

I put some ads up on Facebook, added up the checks, and padlocked the door.
I told George that I was talking to some hot video cam girl about the virus.

Really, I was eating nectarines with them, listening to Fleetwood Mac with them,
playing rummy with them, rifling through my father's death cards with them: for 50 an
hour.

A professor of mine signed on one day. He asked me to watch While You Were Sleeping while his wife napped. He showed me pictures of potatoes he planted before the quarantine.

"Tell me about your father," I said.
"No," he said, "*I* know *you*."

Alyssandra Tobin

I've Been Sheltered I've Been Distanced

Yesterday was my first earthquake if you can believe it the couch shook me back & forth I thought I was having some kinda all-encompassing agita but nope turns out the earth was rending its bones to particles how reasonable.

I've been eating too many beans. Not enough fruits. Have developed some kinda ill-shaped fear around scurvy.

I called my nana she said, "When my family was comin ovah they made em go through health tests at that place, what's it called? That place in New York?" & I said, "Ellis Island?" & she said "Ya, thanks chick. If ya had even a sniffle they locked ya up in this big room. Didn't let ya go nowhere."

I've laughed at my cat's overbite more than twice. Which of course makes her slash my feet for her particular sorta vengeance.

My auntie was there with my nana she said, "Middle of a pandemic, the Manchestah cops still spend all day gahding the beach makin sure only Manchestah residents get to step foot on that rich people sand can you believe it Manchestah is shit." Which, true.

Painted art from *Marriage of Heaven and Hell* into an old mirror. Evil is excess energy. I sleep too much & am always having malformed dreams.

I can't go home for Easter which means no raviolis for the ravioli queen. I'll make my own pizzagaina & have only Aidan to share it with. All that heavy pie for two. Times are dark.

On the phone my ma says "If somebody coughs on me I'll punch em in the face" & I see the chain of inheritance & ancestry solid then tell her "That's one way to get the virus on your hands."

This guy from my high school texts me asking if I remember sitting together in 7th grade math class. "Yeah," I say. "Why." He says, "Aly I'm so fucked up but will you watch a video of me punching myself in the balls?" I say nope & block him. Worry that maybe he wanted me to be meaner.

It's too bad though the guy's hot as hell. He was like this in high school too it's not just cuz quarantine.

The ball torture thing not the hot thing. No one's hot in high school.

Don't worry my ma's read *The Body Keeps the Score*. What she thinks of it is another matter.

Maybe I coulda had him pay me to watch the video. I don't think I'm cut out for that though I have issues with boundaries. I could spit jargon at you all the goddamn day.

One of my students died in a car crash so it says DECEASED next to his name on our online roster. I'd seen him just three days prior. He hissed at me in the hall & when I whipped around looking mad just said "I can't pronounce your name."

Then today I was driving & saw a new white cross with loud red flowers & his name painted in fresh black paint & it's hovering over me now like some bland, persistent gull.

I cried for the first time in months over a goddamn anime. An anime about two boys with super powers got me releasing repressed familial pain. (Scene where a boy holds his little sister close & says "I've been a bad big brother I'm so sorry I promise I will never leave again").

If I told that to my ma she'd scoff me right outta town. "You think you have trauma?" She'd say. "I'll show you trauma." Then she'd recount it all in vicious detail same way she has before & before & before.

I hear unsavory noises at the door. It's not just me don't worry my cat hears them too. Our ears both ringing.

The ivy is falling off my walls. The weird noises are always one of my many neighbors. I think I am failing everyone & everything.

But I mean it's like my nana said: "When the neighbors come to my door I just tell em to get back, ya know we gotta keep some kinda distance."

Tom Bailey

TREATISE ON LONELINESS

It's easy enough to be alone. Just watch: here I am, alone on the sofa; and here now, chopping tofu up in slices. When I found myself alone last week, I stood at the window in my fluffy slippers, watching November have its way with the ash trees outside. A squawk of blue jays came and clattered off. That night, I lay in the bath with my ears underwater, sounding each eardrum for the gusting of blood. Maybe being alone is this: stirring the smaller noises of yourself. Being lonely, though, is harder: it's more than a difference of words. The loneliness gets everywhere, invisible and groaning. You hear it in the fridge's aquatic hum, the radiator's gargle. Last time I was lonely, the flat was cold and terrible, so I slept inside the airing cupboard instead, making a nest of eiderdown and pillows. I curled up under the clothes rack and tried to keep the loneliness out of my lungs, letting the walls close in and hold my body. When that didn't work, I filled the kitchen sink with soil and gathered up my loneliness in handfuls. As night fell, I planted it and listened for the first murmur of growth. When I woke, the kitchen was full of its flowers, tendrils reaching over the stove, the kettle smothered by white blossom. And the sound of a partridge cooing at day's break; the downy breathing of recent buds; fluttering of wings.

Tyler Mills

ISOLATION

I want to go to a New Wave café and sip a cortado
        from a chipped glass cup

while Fugazi crackles from a record and a tuft of hair
        tumbles across the floor, blown by a box fan,

and I want to wipe the sugar cookie crumbs that fell
        from someone else's lips like prayers

to the table with the pad of my palm, and it will be late
        afternoon, a dark day, but the sun

will start to rake the greasy windows and spark the dust
        in the air like gnats hovering over grassy earth,

and a friend will sit down next to me in the empty
        chair and give me a paper bag of her clothes—

I'll pull a webbed sweater over my forehead and nose
        and breathe in her scent (salt, wine, and orchids)—

and she'll ask how the coffee is, and I'll say,
        and she'll press her fingers to the neck,

tapping the invisible prints my skin sweat on the glass,
mingling the marks with hers, with the hours.

David Harsent

Fermata

Silence over silence, stillness over stillness, locked off –
what a held breath gives back, the immensity between
heartbeats… The wind folds into itself, unheard; wavebreak
stalls, unheard; words unspoken return as empty echoes.

Your garden is the world at large. A bird marks the outer edge
and sheers off; the pond carries a shudder: feverish; a fox
turns away, hackles up, wild-eyed. A place where touch
is risk: a rat-trap to rats; to moths, a killing-jar.

You might set a fire only to find that fire is a soundless thing.
You might try music and music be what sight is to the blind.
You want to leave: your first step has already failed.
You want to cry out: that sound is stitched to your tongue.

The silence is the silence of bones, a night-flower, the absence
of something long forgotten, the lost language of stones…
A day…another day…. Too late. Go to the window. Your face
looks back at you. The horizon has come to your gate.

Derek Mahon

QUARANTINE

The privileged crowd in the *Decameron*, avoiding
plague in town, beguiled the days recounting
stories scurrilous and profane; but we can't
amuse ourselves like these since virtual
quarantine is in force against the dreaded virus.
Here we sit, each of us in seclusion, writing
verse and reconciled to an indefinite wait.

What started it, some rogue bacterium indignant
at our plant-genetic drive? Some botched
experiment, some initiative dreamt up by a
special bio-ops dream team? Pneumonic flu is
here and we have to cope but there's no need to
abandon hope for this presages, maybe, a new
age averse to conflict and financial rage.

It's silver-lining time now that the vague threat
represented by the *tourist* plague recedes and the place
is dozing once again in its narcotic haze of drizzling
rain with much-reduced commerce and circumstance
and even a bit of peace for once. Bad news, though,
from abroad: so many stricken, and buried with scant
ceremony

as in pre-modern times, as in *La Peste*. Buried
disease irrupts out of the past: 'Dormant for
years in linen and furniture', it sends its rats
to die in the open air. Some human agent? Nature
getting back at human agency? An ambulance
goes wailing up the road as a stoic shopper
emerges into the eerie silence.

Confined to quarters because coughs, sneezes and
even shared spaces spread diseases, we turn to
Exodus and *The Seventh Seal*, to Nashe and book
six of Lucretius: 'Bad germs invade the
atmosphere so we pick up infection as we inhale.'
A shrill wind whistles above the houses; a briny
stench blows from the roaring shore.

The Dead and the Dying

Mary Noonan

ARITHMOMANIA

The magpies are walking in single file
on the highway. I want to call out,
ask them why they are so many,
but the vowels and consonants rattle,
like loose change, in the purse of my mouth.

The piebald undertakers look like they're
counting – seeds, grains, whatever falls off
the backs of trucks clattering along the road.
Trucks and birds are the only sounds we hear now,
and vocal cords have withered.

I make no sound when I try to say 'hello'
to the old man I see bent before a garden gate.
The cries of unseen children playing have
levered the gut punch, and tears are falling
from his eyes – I count them, keep well back.

He says the dead are laid in neat rows at the ice rink;
I myself have heard army trucks rumbling through
the streets at midnight, ferrying coffins to the next city.
Vampires have returned, reawakened to a world
where counting is all that matters, where

a man in a black tie appears daily on our screens
to sanction our obsession: the number of breaths,
the number of particles in a breath, the number of
millimetres a breath can travel… Vampires will count
anything, and night after night, they relieve the magpies,

slope along the highways, singing the day's numbers.

Rigoberto González

Pandemic, Mon Amour

This is not the poem in tercets that I wanted.
I'm not pleased with its slanted rhymes or that title on it.
Maybe I can switch to a sestina, or better yet, a sonnet.

This is the poem I wrote while in quarantine.
Lockdown took my concentration but by day thirteen
I had mastered the oven and the washing machine.

At first, I worried about meaningless shit like will I
ever visit Greece? Without a gym how can I exercise?
I stressed about getting laid, until my friends died.

One was a novelist, the other a poet. Their names
absorbed by data. I cried into the title pages
of their books. I pressed the dampness to my face

because I had to save some tears for later grief.
The park across my building has begun to green.
This calming view gets shattered every time a wailing

siren lunges at the street. And once again I'm blank,
the desk flatlines right before me. I'm incapable of link-
ing words that can be audible behind the mask

of the computer screen. What stupid metaphors.
I can't escape the lingo of the plague, mon amour.
I'm stuck in 2020. Take me back to pre-COVID-19.

Rachael Allen

from IN SILENCE, MEN FIGHT IN THE OLD TOWN SQUARE

tropic splat
not a cactus
not a TV
but where the body is dumped
this hole in the ground
hair in this kingdom
comes dug from the scalp
come out from the hole
you've been digging
in the blur
in silence, men fight
in the old town square
the hotel doubles
as a hospital
the hole in the ground
is an operating table
made from arguments
made from bone

Alan Shapiro

TODAY

I saw a homeless man beg spare change from another homeless man
who with ratty blanket tied round his neck like a cape
hurried by, head down,
as if he hadn't heard.

I saw a box store at the far end of an empty parking lot
look like it had wakened,
dazed and aphasic, to a geometric nightmare
of an impervious void.

I saw an ambulance
speed through a five-way intersection
without the siren blaring,
while its lights flashed red and yellow pantomimes
over plate glass and brick
which shrugged them off
like something they were just about to think
and then thought better of.

I saw reflected in the highest windows
colossal bodies
of purest white piled
on top of one another toppling
over at their thickest
back to wisps
that thinned to vacancies more blue
for the brief respite.

As if word had gotten out
that there were less of us
and those who remained
were disappearing,
birds suddenly appeared
from who knows where, fearful,
wary, one or two

at first, and then a few more,
and still more, not yet quite
fully trusting
this sudden
spaciousness
until all shapes and sizes sang
from ledges, wires, fence posts, trees, and gutters
in a racket of such rejoicing
so voluptuously shrill so
almost pleasing
it was like hearing every note of a perfect song
played all at once
so all you ever hear of it is noise.

Maya C. Popa

Signal

"To exchange signals with Mars—without fantasizing, of course—
that is a task worthy of a lyric poet."
— Osip Mandelstam

Of course, the secret aim
of losing you those months
had been to find you again.

I went looking for what
had once belonged to you,
found a voice to cauterize

the wound. I made it through
April, May, June; it seemed
I had outsmarted grief

but pulled the hanged man
card repeatedly—the self-same
sorrow said a different way.

You who cannot hear me
without injury, I whisper,
I damage the throat like this,

I, my own entrapment
and hardest to forgive.
Only this life still and all

its boxes filled, its hours
spent fretting over living wills,
the horror of numbers

and headlines on Mars—
more water, more life
where it cannot be touched.

Adam Crothers

Fiona Rae: *Untitled (emergency room)*

oh lie black master
in the lung under

the sketchy thumbnail
lie in my heart meat

me in the morning
but in the end you

climb into bed with
a glint in your hand

place your mouth over
the pillow hold it

suffer a little
come into a child

I know not whatnot
and cannot cando

distribute candies
hang sacks from branches

fly as pennants flayed
flyskin bottleblue

water too blue bright
we love your line its

flat delivery
the good doctor negs

who shuts the shutters
who killed the deadlock

contagion you give
and ever let give

born in the close woods
where dark matter lives

Laura Potts

YESTERDAY'S CHILD

The sun slit a knife through the womb-wet night
and bled like an egg, like a budburst head.
In the swell of the sweat on the belly of the bed,
broken-throated then and red, you said
the clench of winter let the roses grow instead.

But time has fled with jenny wren and left
the meadow dead. And overhead a mouth of moon
has called the mourning on this room, and soon
an ever-bloom of moss will clot the loss of you.
For the years between us are wide as a child,

and the tears as wet as a wound.

Sadbh Kellet

CHRYSEIS

My father prayed for a plague
On the Greeks when their king held
His prize like a broken beast.
His god culled choking choirs
That moaned still in smoking piles
And the beach blackened with ash.
Agamemnon did not stir.
I lay in the king's chamber
Limp like those lifeless bodies
Asking whose death was better?

Breda Spaight

ANCHOR

Then morning again. The sun rises over Keeper Hill silent
as an eye: sunrise, a misnomer — everything is changed
and language still speaks of an old god. The shadow
on the lawn shows there's a crow on the roof. All the gods
are silenced: the sky without a contrail; no tuck . . .
tuck-tuck turnover of a neighbour's car engine; even
the motorway's pebble-rain noise is gone. All changed.
The cherry blossom is in bloom a week early, following
the warmest January in a century, a watercolour of magenta,
fuchsia and cerise that weeps into the quiet of a planet
numbed by a virus. Mug of tea in my hand, I stand
on the deck, its guardrail like the balcony of that hotel
we honeymooned in — Rome. All the bodies
were the same until his smell spoke, clothes aired
where bread was baked — he knew who he was, and his heat
next to mine is still an anchor. Some things don't change.
I'm afraid. Images of the elderly on the screen
every night, leathery fingers tangled, curled
like birds' feet. The frailty that awaits — if I survive
the cancers, bad luck and now this. After the wrinkles,
after the aching joints, names and their faces lost, after
being stripped of my familiar self, who will I be
when all I can do is sit? I step back
into the house. The television jabbers among
last night's wine glasses on the sink, the red roses
in a terracotta jug. Drone footage displays a grid
of fresh graves; charcoal, tan and desert shades of soil
woven, beautiful as an Aztec tapestry, the earth open for all
the beloved and all the forgotten.

Sighle Meehan

Bóthar na Mine

*Bóthar na Mine (Irish): Meal Road. The road was built during
the Great Famine relief works (19th century); the workers were paid in meal.*

Yesterday we dug and cleared,
pruned roses, fertilized the grass.
Everything will grow with love, I promised.
I tied a baby blanket round your shoulders,
blue, trailing like a cloak
and you were Elsa, princess with magic powers
blowing kisses into every corner
calling every frozen thing to green.

Yesterday we found where Spring
had settled in a sunny spot,
shared rice cakes, watched a robin peck the crumbs,
cupped our un-washed hands, drank water
from the outdoor tap.
Today the gate is closed.
You stand outside, your words tossed
by a March wind, an empty double-decker bus.

I know this script.
Potato stalks bloom healthy,
overnight the tubers black and putrid.
Everywhere the stench of rot.
Famine herds my children onto coffin ships,
leaves me to parley with Fever,
I smell his rotten teeth, feel
his yellow hand about my throat.
My brothers build a road to nowhere,
beneath the buses and the speed ramps
their skeletons still hack.

Do the same winds blow forever, the same script
always? Or if I distance, if I wave
with empty arms, can I force the ending?
You wear your cloak, weave a spell
love-kissed daisies splurge the lawn
we thread a garland, our bodies close.

Olga Dugan

Liminal Spaces

"The threshold is God's waiting room." -Richard Rohr
(for Craig)

seems he'd lain there
a year and a lifetime's worth
of gin of self-pity
friends find him slumped over
half on the sofa
head a great weight
against the coffee table
hand stretching past it
phone just out of clutch

MIA from work two days
silence slapping friends
who turn the cheek
soon as they read
his body's stillness
as confession
sickness having grayed
and thinned his hair
browns skin to their touch
like the fallen peaches
rotting his yard
they wonder what other road
had taken his heart
to this thicket and what
path they should brave
to meet and bring it home

emergency answers their call
tests show drinking
corroded kidneys
COVID did the rest
invading infecting clotting lungs
collapsing one

but somewhere between there
and several months of repair
he tells family friends
he'd found a road
not taken since he thought
as a child behaved as a child
a hope
to hear once more

his front door whine open
to rake his yard
once more
against an ever-lighter
blue and periwinkle dawn
to spray his peach trees
setting the stage for growth
when the weather was appropriate
once more

his body wracked and wrecked
could muster neither will
nor way to carry him home
but this faith he tells us
the same that woke him
from two successful surgeries
from years of crippling doubt
reminded him of his boyhood
God Who cared and now
he knows could

The New Normal

Kim Moore

If Some God Shakes Your House

"but if some god shakes your house
ruin arrives
ruin does not leave"
                    ANNE CARSON

And when some god or other
reached down and took our house
between its hands
and also our neighbour's house
and our neighbour's neighbour's house,
shaking them back and forth
in the same way you might rock
a stubborn plant to ease it
from the soil,
when we felt not the hands
of the god around us
but its mouth,
it was then that ruin arrived,
hiding in the smallest spaces
but also multiplying,
riding out with us
on our hair and clothes,
we had faces of ruin,
we had the breath and hands of ruin,
we wore the garments of ruin,
ruin was in our eyes
and though now it is weeks
since we began to live with ruin
and eat at table with its anger,
weeks since we slept with ruin
in our beds, I promise you,
my dear ones, we do not have
hearts of ruin, ruin cannot survive
inside our hearts.

Sandra Beasley

THIS IS THE WAY THE WORLD _____

Grass cells, placed under the microscope, appear to smile.
I'd like for joy to be so embedded in the world,
as I watch a child's birthday party gather by the duck pond—
six children, six sets of parents, spaced equidistant
around circumference. They wave at each other. I watch
from the window of an apartment that I haven't left in a week.

The pandemic tastes like parsley, which the Italian restaurant
now our grocery store gave us four great big bags of:
parsley as salad, parsley-potato soup, chopped
by handful over the chicken. Sometimes joy is picking away
rotty bits, nestling what remains in paper towels
to stretch two more days. The birthday boy tests his balloon's

tether of curling-ribbon, debating. He's turning six, maybe seven.
Young enough to watch ducks lift into sky and return to Earth,
not realizing his balloon makes no such promise.
Or maybe he just doesn't want to watch it pucker and decay
back in the safety of home; maybe
he'd rather watch his friends clap as it escapes for good.

I'm old enough to realize someone manipulated the photograph
of cells, contrasting yellow against green, adding blue
to lift those smiley maws to the surface,
yet still the grass is grinning.
I trace parsley's name back to Latinized Greek for *stone*,
insistent among rock. We take our joys where we find them.

Brian Turner

Painting History in the Sky

I'll tell you what—the suburbs are never boring
on Pandemia. My neighbor says, "I got extra clips
if you're short on ammo." He's afraid
the night-screams we hear over the treetops
will come running down our street, all
burning with agency and headed for his life,
his wife, his angry little dog that barks
as if it might startle the flowers into bloom.

Across the street, the red-faced man remains
pregnant with beer and forty-odd years
of always being right. He put a flag on a flagpole,
draped another over his fence, then painted his Jeep
in the national colors. The blades of grass
keep rising up green, and sometimes I see him
out late at night with a tiny paintbrush, fixing it all,
on his knees there in the moonlight, making it right.

During the seasonal pandemics, we all put buckets
out in the yard. The storms bring an ocean of tears
that come down icy and cool, so cool all the little kids
run in circles and laugh as their exhausted parents
lean their heads back to close their eyes, to reminisce
on days gone by. We'll have to boil the water after—
to separate the pain from the sadness, the overwhelming
grief from the occasional joy that rains down in sheets.

And I watch it all through the giant glass windows
in the living room. The neighbors, needing a hobby,
pumped water into my house to make an aquarium
for their amusement. They know I'm a writer
and so they like to watch me floating as words
float on the pages around me, my pen sometimes
just out of reach, the way clouds drift over Pandemia
like billboards with promises of calamities to come.

When I open the front door it's like being reborn—
the day shot through with sunlight, the streets
washed clean with tears that took generations
to gather and pour over the rooftops and cities
of Pandemia. My dog smiles at everyone. She
doesn't speak the language, so she doesn't know
the things they say to one another, but she sees
the gestures, the minute overtures, love in its halting starts.

At dusk, the ice chests open and the red-faced man ignites
fireworks into the air above our street. The little kids
thrill to the sparkling little wars exploding above them,
the nostalgia of it painted so brilliantly it brings a hush
to everyone there. It's enough to send us all off to dream
while the neighbor's dog barks and barks at the flowers,
though the flowers, filled with enough sunlight and tears—
they keep their petals pulled tight to the bulb.

They know. Tomorrow will never be the same.

Moya Cannon

Taking the Brunt of It

I pick them up in the sunny park every morning,
to bring home and put in a glass jug.
They are mostly short-stemmed,
bent and broken by April gusts.
I did not know there were so many different kinds —
orange fringed suns, yellow trumpets,
dainty white dancers, saffron flouncers.

The brave narcissi, up
and out on strong green stems,
lifting their heads to the sun,
taking the brunt of spring storms —
a few young ones snap at the root
but, mostly, it's the older ones,
with weakened stems,
which bend and break.

In this storm which rips across the world,
which has grounded air fleets,
and emptied teeming streets,
it's the older ones,
who sit, heads nodding,
in tall-backed chairs,
who smile into the phone,
so many different beloved ones,
who take the brunt of it.

Paula Cunningham

Some Things I Am Finding on Zoom®
April 2020

That the yellow frame is a poor indicator of interest
      How nobody knows what goes on in the Waiting Room
That waving and meaningful peering are equally futile
How muteness may be selected or imposed
That the layout of every participant's panes will differ in Gallery View
How nobody ever knows who owns the blackbird
That people in rural Tyrone are frequently frozen
      How to gaze past the edge of the screen is to enter confession
That you, without question, are leading the crawl to accomplish a multiple chin
That there's chicken skin on my neck I might never have noticed
How I cannot, now, unknow this
      How, in our times, we've never felt this seen
That the eye is less deniable than the ear
      How the griefs we're avoiding are loitering north of the screen

Greg Rappleye

Social Distances

During the first days of the Corona pandemic
I often sat in a chair near the road, smoking cigarettes,
half a mile south of a group-home that had become
infested with the virus. Three, maybe five times
a week, the shiny blue ambulance that serves
those who live north of the lift-bridge hustled by, siren
wailing, red, white-and-amber lights awhirl, and turned
into the group-home parking lot. It became the habit
of an older man from the rental cottages across the way
to stand on his side of the road, in a wool overcoat
and surgical mask, hand over his heart, waving
a small flag as the amulance raced back toward the bridge
and the ventilators that chuffed beyond.
One terrible day, after the ambulance made the last
of three deadly runs (it's said that only two of ten
who went on the vents survived), I called over to him,
after he'd stepped all the way to the pavement
to watch the ambulance make the final curve and the ramp
that leads to the far shore. He hesitated, then walked
back to his cottage. I haven't seen him out since,
though from time-to-time I see what may be a hand
waving slowly, or a half-smile in the tiny window
cut in his cottage door.

Afric McGlinchey

LEAN SEASON

Either that or I'm a boat.
Usually I feel whoosh.
Cut down the bookcase, bottles of whiskey.
That's how a car drives down here, very west cork.
I'm laughing because you should see what they say
when they stop you: Cove 19.
The tide is a dog in the lap.
In a week, a minute, he turns into a mental pygmy
and I get to be the grumpy
old man at the pier – that's my next career move.

Every tall dog operates on her hips, gets lots of loving.
More than an hour, including two, even four times;
you might get a chance.
I was vaguely aware of the lads,
and a courting couple last summer.
Enough company can fall right through.
Regulars and children are a quick red rock,
checking the slip.
I'll sit down to look at the bottles of wine.
Three's the alarm.

These are therapy dogs – warmer and drier than my pipe and net
or any pretty skills. One had cancer in her ear.
Legs on the sill and white;
no substitute for days when you're busy.
Oh dear god.
This rage comes from nowhere, into position.
A hot workshop, where I suggest eggs.
They all recognise a car.
Fachtna the postman spilling lollies,
and Miller spilling joy.

A fly gets arrested while I stand above
at the garda checkpoint.
It's all to do with the torches. I have the west cork works.
On the busiest mornings, they scarper.

Two had a barbecue on the boat.
The most expensive, of course, are never any good
At the minute, I can't eat all the mackerel people bring me.
A minimum of six in these stricken years.
The last hour will give you the nod.
Would love to go bonkers, clear out the summer.

It's howling outside, hence the one ear.
I was silent all night, and what the fuck, I owe him.
He'll take on an accent, come roaring into four legs.
When kids ask, I say you should see how the other dog looked.
Toby was always just enough
to raise me up in the mornings, after Luke died .
Even water, even your mentor can be frozen.
Conscious of someone outside the scene.
It's payback time. Nothing is amiss.
Look after yourself. It's lovely to see you.

WJ Herbert

Tibetan Singing Bowls

I cling, mask-less in nightmares,
to a subway's center pole

as the car hurls sparks through
a jumble of dark tunnels.

The car, whose doors won't
open, barrels on as unmasked

people sneeze, charging the air
with particles. I don't die

but wake, hyperventilating.
And, so, every morning

I listen to bowls sing
so that when night comes

again, Cerberus will stop me
from passing through

shadowy gates. Though
to guard me was never his

charge, he must hear vibrations
singing inside me.

But how do the bowls
convince my body's wandering

blood to ferry their
mysterious hymns?—

How, in the body's maze,
do they say: *Breathe.*

Patrick Holloway

Don't forget to love

Wash your hands,
Show them love as your fingers
Fold in on each other. Enjoy the water
Rinsing away what lingers. Wash away too
Those negative thoughts that build up like walls.
Sing. To your loved ones, out windows, let your voice echo.
Make calls. Send voice messages and memes. Laugh.
Open that bottle of wine, put on your favourite album
And dance, swirling your glass, your body. Wash your hands
Again, this time to the music. Find the Monopoly board with missing
Pieces. This will lead to fights which will lead to normality, temporarily.
Do not pass go. Do what's right, not just for you but for that old lady
Who lives across the street. Leave groceries at her door.
Send nice long emails. Read. All those books you never get round to
Taking off the shelf. Devour them. Read poetry. Write.
Anecdotes, jokes, stories, messages, novels and love letters.
Be better. Wash your hands again. Help others wash away
Any racism or xenophobia. Teach. About safety but also about life.
Lessons learned that can help. Listen. To each other, to the silence,
To the birds and barking of neighbouring dogs. Stay active. Jumping
Jacks and Yoga. Breathe. Three deep breaths when those negative thoughts
Come back. Then wash them away again. Set up Skype calls with all your
Friends who live abroad, with no way of visiting home. Share.
Toilet paper and alcohol gel and your thoughts and worries, share them
With others. Binge watch Netflix. Wash your hands. Don't touch your face
As beautiful and itchy as it may be. Care for yourself, for your family,
For the stranger you pass by every day on your way to work.
Stay at home. Even if you think you don't need to.
Wash your hands. Stay safe. Smile.

Martín Veiga

A RESPIRACIÓN

Lento respira el mundo en mi respiración
ANTONIO COLINAS

Escribir coma quen tenta atopar a respiración
do mundo agora que o alento se perde
entre os intersticios do que xa non son
nin talvez xamais serei, polas regañas
mais ocultas da alma, onde se abeira o riso,
o fulxir da disidencia, os misterios do amor.
Atopar así nos protocolos da escrita
un motivo para que carrizos e xílgaros
rechouchíen ao mencer, para que retorne
a vida a iluminar coa súa grilanda de luz
todos os camiños que agora permanecen
no escuro, as congostras cegas deste país
cuxas fronteiras son móbiles, están feitas
de auga que percute en cantís sonámbulos,
en rochedos grises, coma a irradiación
dunha enerxía tan voraz que non se inscribe
tan só nas pedras enfouladas da mariña,
senón que penetra na cerna, no abismo
máis profundo que me dita, ourizo pecho
de castaña ou tobo fondo de furón furtivo.
Porén, habítame ao escribir estas palabras
un silencio feble no que apenas se percibe
a respiración do mundo a asolagar o mundo,
o ritmo pausado da respiración do mundo
a achegar ás augas o corazón dos cervos.

The Breath

Slowly breathes the world in my breath
Antonio Colinas

Writing like someone who is after the breath
of the world now its spirit has fallen
between the spaces of what I once was
and may never be again, through the hidden
chasms of the soul that shelter laughter,
the glow of dissent and the mysteries of love.
Revealing in the craft the reason wrens
and goldfinches trill to the dawn, so life
turns again to festoon with its light
all those dark ruts, all those blind
holloways criss-crossing this country
of fluid frontiers; the water
beating against somnambulant cliffs
and grey rocks, like the irradiation
of an energy so voracious it doesn't just etch
itself onto the spindrifted seastacks
but penetrates down to the core,
to my guiding abyss, the clamped
chestnut burr, the ferret's furtive burrow.
However, writing these words a silence
takes over where I can scarcely feel
the world's breath flooding the world,
the calm rhythm of the world's breath
as the deer's heart nears the water.

Translated from Galician by Keith Payne

John McAuliffe

TESTING, TESTING

If after long silence
                  the voice

at the other end
of the line

offers
           Aberdeen International Airport

and the home page
              (refreshed, refreshed)

does not change
                  like the curve rising

towards where
                the trees

nowhere near
Aberdeen International Airport

lay down
              their reds and yellows

at the slightest
gust from the west

will we instead
             and why not

do what we did
             when we said

we were
           going fishing

Patrick Deeley

The Flea-Catcher

Is she praying, her knuckles pressed against
each other? No, she's crushing a flea
between her thumbnails. You can almost hear
the click as the abdomen bursts.

It's what we did as children. And the candle,
we had that, too. Its flame rose
straight up, as in this painting –
all but anticipating the tiny, squashed corpse

which we would feed to it. Nothing
in our action disgusted us:
we simply dreaded the flea for the sickness
its bite could transmit. Now,

in a season of fresh plague, I discover again
how viscerally intimate
is the world, the very meat
and breath of it capable of carry or crossover,

but witness given to the good that's risen
even out of this latest misfortune
sustains me as I sit quarantined,
gazing at a book opened on the *tenebroso* art

of Georges de la Tour – and then
I see a simple wooden chair in a small room
where the light and dark
of our childhood dramas startlingly contend.

Gerard Smyth

Rising Tide

The buses are empty but still on their way
to Stocking Lane and Limekiln Avenue or back
to city centre, then on to the airport north of there.

There is time to count old mistakes, learn the tricks
of solitaire, and on days the mercury rises
we step outside to see the ways the garden heals

itself with lavender and yellow broom.
The back room gets the last of the evening sun,
so we sit there and become sun-worshippers.

Or we switch on the TV but don't know
what we're looking for: the triviality of a soap opera,
the chat show host who can coax a secret or a story?

We watch the news but mute the sound
when the loudmouth from *La La Land* comes on
with all his make-believe, propagating falsehoods.

Perhaps like the birds we should read the sky
and not the headlines that hit us like a clenched fist,
or drown us in their rising tide of black ink.

Audrey Molloy

LOCKDOWN BOOGIE

Let's go dancing, in our heads.
You take my hand, I toss the rose.
We mustn't kiss, we both agree
that would be irresponsible.
Can you hear that slide guitar?
No. I can hear a mandolin —
but certainly, the blues.
We've waded through discarded masks
like leaf-litter in the alley
and stumbled down the stairway
to the Blind Tiger in our minds.
The barman ties his paisley scarf
like a highwayman's disguise,
while he mixes your Negroni
and, for me, a mauve concoction
he calls the Amelia Earhart.
He dips the rim of a conical glass
first in egg white, then fine sugar,
and you whisper of a masked ball
between the wars, a faceless, silent
party; how they wove their spells:
the contour where velvet meets throat,
the barest brush of a lace cuff,
and, despite our best intentions,
your mouth works its way up my arm,
a tentacle passing delicacies along
the conveyor belt of its pale hoops,
and when you reach my neck
I tilt my head. And, reader,
you don't know if *towards* or *away*
but will just have to imagine.

Lani O'Hanlon

Sound

In the mornings Miriam takes her son Peter out in a small yellow dinghy.
He lies across it on his tummy, legs sticking out like a swallow's tail
dip into the water, then back into the air, as she pushes him across the bay.

Craft sail from the beach below the church in Abbeyside
to the Cunnigar. The sea this morning like corrugated iron,
no break in the clouds. Miriam wades through seaweed.

In time, he will learn to row despite what the neurologists say.
The rhythm of the waves is within, his people were fishermen.
His fear of loud noise, his roars, quieted here.

She walks, pushes, he leans his cheek on the side of the dinghy
the sea passing through and beneath them, all the way to Helvic.

Karen's boy Derek would never sleep as a baby, unless
she had the *Hoover* running or a hairdryer. She burnt out
three hairdryers and two *Hoovers* putting him to sleep.

Such a big baby, the dome of his head covered in a fuzz of blonde,
round blue eyes. She was only nineteen pushing the pram away
then back towards her, away and back, then rocking rocking;

in the sitting room with the swirly patterns; a rented house in Tallaght.
The noise reminded me of our mother in a temper cleaning. Over the hum
we chatted, drank instant coffee, a cream slice for me, a doughnut for her.

Now Derek is a young man trying to breathe in intensive care. The sound
of the ventilator will soothe him, the deep sea, the sound of the womb.

Paul Mariani

Covid Boogie

Some guy swaggers into a supermarket without a mask
and a father, mask on with his little masked daughter
beside him, asks him to cover up or leave, as he oughta
to maintain some social distance, when suddenly the guy takes
a step away, pulls out a Glock from the back
of his belt, and points it at the father's head, then is heard to say
he don't like being threatened, so back off, Jack, O.K?

An old woman—maskless--bumbles into some discount store
and a young woman employee —masked—rushes over
to explain that masks are store policy, and so needs to ask
her to obey the rules. She even offers the woman a free mask
while she's inside shopping, something for her own safety
as well as everyone's, even as customers go buzzing by
hunting for toilet paper and whatever else they're looking for.

But the old woman ain't having none of it. Says she has rights
too, guaranteed by Uncle Sam and the U.S.S. Constertution.
And to make her point, decides to plop herself down in the main
aisle until at last the manager himself comes over to explain
it's his duty to keep his customers safe. But no, she fights
stubbornly on, until finally she pushes herself up and wobbles her way
outside, middle finger up, then flings the mask by way of retribution.

August 2020. Three quarters of a million bikers, tattoo-
branded maskless bearded faces, descend once more on Sturgis,
South Dakota. And this being the real West, they mean to urge us
all to make America great again, the way it was, when Fort
Meade made its mark and Deadwood made another. Despite
the warnings of ten thousand doctors, though, here they are, hordes
of leather jackets, dungarees, and T-shirts reading "Screw

Covid, I went to Sturgis." Rebel flags, here, there, everywhere,
mixed with banners proclaiming "Don't tread on me" to make it clear.
And then there's guns and weed and topless chicks and beer,
adding up to brawls and crashes by the score, and more.
Masks, they sneer, are for dumb-ass liberals like me and you.
And didn't their main man Trump say this Covid thing's a flu?
Something he told us a shot of hydroxychloroquine would cure?

And on and on it goes, the wrecking numbers racking up each day
as now college kids like those I taught head back to school
mixing Zoom and social distance classes, then head out to sway
to hip-hop strobe light gatherings at night as they share drool
and then they're tested and find they've caught it too (no way,
baby, this can't be!) and like that truth hits them between the eyes
and it's goodbye college, as all (or much of what) they hoped for dies.

Meanwhile ambulances wait in empty parking lots, one more stifled cough
echoing eerily by the ER entrance as drivers wait for the inevitable next call.
Think now, she said, think now of that *indescribable sorrow that follows*
every lonely last breath when the ventilators at last turn off.
Think too of our loved ones alone. Think of those final swallows
as the blue-lipped face turns up, the eyes, face fitted to a metal shawl,
think of that mad captain dancing us down death's dark empty hall.

Anthony Walton

CORONA

I

They say the virus is in China, in Boston, in Brunswick
down the street—

they say it is next door—it is somewhere
and nowhere

2

Whatever it is I thought I was, I am
empty: the neighborhood
of myself, empty

suburban streets, commercial avenues
inside me are empty and full
of fear—

3

They say that the virus is to be respected—

that it is like a cold, like the flu, that there is nothing
to it except a hoax.

Some say it is the end of the world.

4

Waiting, for silence, for the negative
of nothing to happen. In hope that nothing
will happen.

When has nothing not happened?

5

Waiting for my loved one to materialize out of lust—

waiting, worried I might not see her again—waiting, worried
that should I see her again, it will be too late, that she will be
somewhere, someone, else—

6

A flicker and glow as when a sun is eclipsed by a moon

eclipse: as if there is only absence, apprehension, waiting

7

The meaning of the word *incipient*—

so much incipience

the news, the test, the negative that could be false, the false
that could be positive

8

The more nothing happens, the better,
the more fear, wonder, worry where are the neighbors—

What is out there, in the empty—

Amlanjyoti Goswami

AT THE END OF TODAY

My mother will shrug off
The oxygen cylinder, the tubes on her nose,
Take out the pin pricks from wrist and arms
Turn the saline upside down
Ask for some fresh clothes, no the usual won't do,
Get me some good Benarsi silk, will you?
And thank the nurses at the counter, wish them a long life
Filled with cherries and tomatoes,
And then come down the weary steps, one at a time,
Dodge the guards who ask where are you going?
Home, can't you see?
And downstairs, even pay the bills herself,
The ones insurance won't allow.
She will refuse the car and instead walk
Through the dust, where cars and refuse get parked,
And ask for the back gate to be opened, just for her.
She will walk out of the gates, in regal pearl,
And turning left, navigate the ups and downs of the footpath
Mirroring life, as if this is San Francisco and not Zoo Road.
Then she will pretend to not see a thing as she travels the distance
Past the empty lot where the street vendors used to be,
Passing the liquor shop, the empty bus stop, the zoo with its monkeys
Hanging from the branches and wishing her luck.
She will cross the parantha shops, the momo shacks, the mutton ghugni joints,
She will hear the whispers of lovers no longer there
She will look for no one, so sure about her destination
And not a bus will stop for her, and the roads are anyway empty these days.
An odd bicycle will brush past her, a curious street dog yelping
And then she will buy medicines herself from the pharmacy closed for all time.
Keep the change, she will say, taking a deep breath, the one denied her for so long.
Then she will turn, left, where the bus stops, where the crowd throngs usually
For the daily gossip. She will take a turn, and walk on, past the doctor's house, now quiet
With those big gates. She will cross the lawyer, the vegetable vendor and the tea shack.
She will wave to the old man on the terrace, drinking his coffee.
Then she will open the gates herself, push them with all her might,
Unlock the grilled bars, and enter, once more, the lonely room where she finds, at last,
place.

Upstairs, the petunias, marigolds, lemons and brinjals on the terrace will ask her for one look
But she will say, later, later. Right now, I have to breathe. Right now there is a house.
Then she will enter her room, the only one, take a deep breath, sigh, and ask
Where was I so long?

Julie Kane

DUPLEX: MINT CHIP

I will not write a pandemic poem
I'll fix another bowl of mint chip ice cream

      I've gained eleven pounds on mint chip ice cream
      Nobody sees my body, so it doesn't count

The last man on earth to see my body
Lied to me about voting for Trump

      Trump voters think the virus is a hoax
      I no longer want him to touch my body

Yoga pants barely touch the body!
Is anyone on Zoom even wearing pants?

      No Trumpster is gonna get into these panties
      Let's make America Puritan again

I hear America's ventilators panting
Deejay Trump's beatbox for pandemic poems

Anthony Lawrence

Daylight Star

The only daylight star I've seen,
　　　　　apart from one that burns
　　　　　　　　　the retina after
reckless exposure, turned out to be
　　　　　the last international flight
　　　　　　　　　before borders closed
like poor theatre doors.
　　　　　I tried to imagine your face
　　　　　　　　　in a window on that
Seven Four Seven, bound for London,
　　　　　although you might have been
　　　　　　　　　at home, moving
from room to room
　　　　　and putting things into boxes.
　　　　　　　　　I'll never know.
Communication and precise location
　　　　　had been abandoned,
　　　　　　　　　as when a transponder
is turned off, unexpectedly.
　　　　　I confused the sound
　　　　　　　　　of packing tape being torn
from its roll with a fighter jet
　　　　　passing over a breakwater,
　　　　　　　　　where we had been
scanning the sky for Sirius and Capella
　　　　　with a pair of binoculars.
　　　　　　　　　I like to bring things closer
than how they first appear:
　　　　　your mouth and eyes, to be
　　　　　　　　　unapologetically sentimental
about it, also the regulated
　　　　　bloom and fade of an artery
　　　　　　　　　in your neck that I loved
to time with my tongue prior to isolation.
　　　　　An airliner gleams and vanishes.
　　　　　　　　　A planet is mistaken for a star.

Maia Elsner

SGT PEPPERS LONELY HEARTS

Before lockdown lifts, there are fishbones & fish,
deep-fried & battered, wrapped in headlines, letter
promises embossed on chips, our greasy wishes
burnt alongside fingertips & tongues, tapering

the red sun squatting down low in imitation of us.
Each evening, our game is this: *can you catch me,*
shadows. Later, the queues outside *Peppers Burgers.*
No social distancing. Only, bodies twirling & we

turn also, to gossip in the graveyard of dead children.
Our deepest secrets fall in between dirty needles,
condoms & corona bottles, like smashed bronze. Again
sweet second-hand weed scent wafts, reminding us

we are not alone. Breathe it in deep. You speak
of dying. I say, *it's going to rain.* I fill the space.

Hope/Between Waves

Aifric Mac Aodha

ATHOSCAILT

Is é an cleas atá ann an righneas mínádúrtha,
an seasamh siar a chur díot láithreach, gan aon riail á sárú.
Má tá tú istigh leo, ní chuirfear cnámh ann.

Caithfidh an fear atá scoite ón mbeár mála Tayto leat
le tabhairt dá shípéir Gearmánach – Dante –
is nuair a fhiafróidh a chompánach de

ar osclaíodh prochóg éigin faoin mbaile mór, an bhfuil oisrí anois á riar acu,
is ar mhaithe leatsa chomh maith le héinne
a labhróidh an guth taobh thiar den chuntar, *Tá sin... oisrí agus super noodles.*

Reopening

The trick will be to slip off the bridle
as soon as you can without breaking the rules. If
you catch it, you'll know in your marrow.

The man ringfenced from the bar will toss you a bag
of Tayto to give to his German shepherd – Dante –
and when his other pal asks if some dive

in town is open, and if they're serving oysters now,
for your benefit as much as anyone else's
the voice from behind the counter will say, *They are… oysters and super noodles.*
translated from Irish by David Wheatley

Nell Regan

MARCH

Light holds out
its arms —
level, steady

*

Bird song
populates the sky
with morning news

I am here, I am here.
Still here.

*

All things
are overtaken
by the bright
of the sea —

that heaving,
breathing
mirror of light.

*

Twice daily
sea cleans down
each surface of the beach.

*

Another empty train
flies by
light on its rails.

Peter Sirr

RENGA

Great is the summer: when the pizzas come, we are already outside

Sun strikes the plant pots that hide the broken window sill: the other is unhidden

The neighbour is on the extension roof again, poking the rusty satellite dish: the world waits

Camden Street deserted: the copper dome floats towards the mountain

Dogs in Covid squaring off, lunging, panting: how do you explain?

Sun warms the gravel then cools again; the red chair waits its turn

Summer winter autumn spring: up at the dog's dawn again

The gardens are open: round and round we go on our extended leads

May: the window open, cherry blossoms on the floor

Mo sits outside her front door, Butterfly weeps around her

The stillest season: the frozen counterweights and jibs of cranes

Ladders unclimbed, loads unlifted: hook, line, silence

Someone turns on the news: the centre folds, the darkness holds

Summer is here, a blatant light, a persistent rumour

The dog jumps in the river: how can you not have told me it was still here?

We walk past the locked up playground: the loudest silence yet

A crowd gathers around the bandstand: a century ago the concert begins

Still open the butcher on Pembroke Street: sausages, paté, a little bread

We walk on empty streets like a photograph of history: the city waits to begin

We walk alive on crowded streets, tripping over people and dogs: closeness is all

From pavements, from walls, from Georgian salons, from fanlights and doors, from tree-tops and canal rushes, from barges and building sites, from avenues and lanes, from cellars and mews they surge; from rooftops and gardens, from rooftop gardens, from terraces and sheds, from balconies, from footholds and towpaths, from greenhouses and barracks the populace presents itself: a reprieve, a retrieval, an interim, an interstice, a lodge for the liminal, an unresting place, you can hardly get in among them, there's scarcely a breath between them, the air is thick with bodies

The city is a wild caress
                    great is the summer

Paste another poem here.

Paste another poem here.

Paste another poem here.

Paste another poem here.

Paste another poem here.

Paste another poem here.

Paste another poem here.

Acknowledgements

With the following exceptions permission to reproduce the poems in this book came from the poets themselves:

The Gallery Press courteously gave permission to reproduce 'Quarantine' by Derek Mahon from his collection *Washing Up* (2020) and 'The Polio Epidemic' by Eiléan Ní Chuilleanáin from her collection *The Sun-Fish* (2009).

Southword Editions gave permission for 'Zoonoses' by John Mee from his chapbook *From the Extinct* (2017).

Biographical Notes

Rachael Allen's first collection of poems, *Kingdomland*, is published by Faber & Faber. She writes for *ArtReview*, *TANK* magazine and *Music & Literature*, hosts the Faber Poetry Podcast and is the poetry editor for *Granta* magazine and Granta books.

Tom Bailey is a poet from the United Kingdom. He studied English Literature at Cambridge University before starting an MFA in Poetry at Boston University. His poems have been published in *The Mays Anthology*, *The Blue Nib*, *The Kindling*, *Lighthouse Literary Journal*, *Hawk & Whippoorwill*, and Allographic's *In Other Words* anthology.

Sandra Beasley grew up in Virginia. She is the author of the poetry collections *Count the Waves* (2015); *I Was the Jukebox* (2010), which won the Barnard Women Poets Prize; and *Theories of Falling* (2008), winner of the New Issues Poetry Prize. She was 2019 John Montague Poetry Fellow.

Paula Bohince is the author of three poetry collections, most recently *Swallows and Waves* (Sarabande Books, 2016). She lives in Pennsylvania. She was 2020 John Montague Poetry Fellow.

Paddy Bushe lives in Waterville, Co. Kerry. He received the 2006 Oireachtas prize for poetry, the 2006 Micheal Hartnett Poetry Award and the 2017 Irish Times Poetry Now Award. He is a member of Aosdána. In 2020, Dedalus Press published *Double Vision,*.

Moya Cannon's sixth collection is *Donegal Tarantella* (2019, Carcanet Press). She was born in County Donegal and lives in Dublin. A winner of the Behan Award and the O'Shaughnessy Award, she has edited Poetry Ireland Review and was 2011 Heimbold Chair of Irish Studies at Villanova University, P.A., USA.

Jane Clarke is the author of two poetry collections *The River* and *When the Tree Falls* (Bloodaxe Books 2015 & 2019) as well as an illustrated chapbook, *All the Way Home*, (Smith|Doorstop 2019).

Patrick Cotter has published three collections, *Perplexed Skin* (Arlen 2008) *Making Music* (Three Spires Press 2009) and *Sonic White Poise* (Dedalus 2021). He is a recipient of the Keats-Shelley Poetry Prize.

Adam Crothers was born in Belfast in 1984, and lives in Cambridge. His first collection, *Several Deer* (Carcanet, 2016), won the 2017 Shine/Strong Poetry Award and the 2017 Seamus Heaney Centre Prize. His second collection, *The Culture of My Stuff*, appeared in 2020

Paula Cunningham lives in Belfast. Her books, both from Smith/Doorstop, are *A Dog called Chance*, and *Heimlich's Manoeuvre*.

Tony Curtis is the author of ten collections of poetry, most recently *New & Selected Poems: From the Fortunate Isles* (Seren, 2016). He has won the Eric Gregory Award, the National Poetry Prize, the Dylan Thomas Award and a Cholmondeley Award. He is Emeritus Professor of Poetry at the University of South Wales where he founded and directed the M. Phil Writing course

Patrick Deeley is a poet, memoirist and children's writer. His seventh collection, *The End of the World*, recently appeared from Dedalus Press. He is the 2019 recipient of the Lawrence O'Shaughnessy Poetry Award. His best-selling memoir, *The Hurley-Maker's Son*, was shortlisted for the 2016 Irish Book of the Year Awards

Olga Dugan is a Cave Canem poet from Philadelphia, Pennsylvania. Nominated for Best of the Net and Pushcart Prizes, her award-winning poems have appeared widely in American journals.

Maia Elsner grew up between Oxford and Mexico City, with stints spent in France and Italy, and began writing poetry while living in Boston, Massachusetts. Her poems have been published in British, American and Canadian journals and in *Un Nueva Sol: British Latinx Writers*.

Martín Espada was born in Brooklyn, New York in 1957. He has published more than fifteen books as a poet, editor, essayist and translator. His latest collection is *Vivas to Those Who Have Failed*

Sophie Ewh is a writer and podcaster living in New York. Her work has been published by The Poetry Society of New York, *The Rational Creature*, WQXR, and several other organizations around NYC.

John Fitzgerald has received the Patrick Kavanagh Poetry Prize and in 2015 was shortlisted for the Hennessy New Irish Writing Award. He is the recipient of a 2015 Key West Literary Bursary and acted as a juror for the 2016 Poem for Ireland Competition. His chapbook *First Cut* (Southword Editions) was published in 2017.

Tom French's first collection *Touching the Bones* (Gallery Press, 2001) was awarded the Forward Prize for Best First Collection, 2002. The Gallery Press has also published *The Fire Step* (2009), *Midnightstown* (2014), *The Way to Work* (2016), *The Last Straw* (2018, Irish Times/ Poetry Now Award shortlist) and *The Sea Field* was published in April 2020.

Rigoberto González is the author of five books of poetry, most recently *The Book of Ruin,* published by Four Way Books. The recipient of Guggenheim, NEA and USA Rolón fellowships, and many awards, including the Lenore Marshall Prize from the Academy of American, he is contributing editor for *Poets & Writers* magazine and writes a monthly column for NBC-Latino online.

Amlanjyoti Goswami's recent collection of poems *River Wedding* (Poetrywala) has been widely reviewed. His poetry has been published in journals and anthologies around the world. His poems have also appeared on street walls in Christchurch, exhibitions in Johannesburg, an e-gallery in Brighton and buses in Philadelphia. He lives in Delhi.

James Harpur has had five poetry collections published by Anvil Press and is poetry editor of the *Temenos Academy Review* and a member of Aosdána. His *Angels and Harvesters* (2012) was shortlisted for the 2013 Irish Times Poetry Now Award; and *The Dark Age* (2007) won the Michael Hartnett Poetry Award

Will Harris is a poet and critic from London. He is the author of the chapbook, *All This Is Implied,* and the essay *Mixed-Race Superman.* His debut collection *RENDANG* was published by Granta in February was a Poetry Book Society Choice and 2020 winner of the Forward Prize for First Collection.

David Harsent has published twelve volumes of poetry, most recently *Salt* (2017), *Fire Songs* (2014), which won the T.S. Eliot Prize, and *Night* (2011), which won the Griffin International Poetry Prize, all from Faber & Faber.

Rachael Hegarty is a Dubliner. She has published three collections. *Flight Paths Over Finglas* (Salmon, 2017) won the Shine Strong Award. *May Day 1974* (Salmon, 2019) and *Dancing with Memory* (Salmon, 2021),

WJ Herbert's chapbook manuscript, *Riddles of Flock & Bone* was chosen by Patricia Smith as finalist for the 2019 Poetry Society of America Chapbook Fellowship. She lives in Kingston, New York. [wjherbertpoet.com.]

Patrick Holloway's story was the winning January story for The Hennessy New Writing Competition. He was the winner of Headstuff poem of the year. He won second place in the Raymond Carver Fiction Contest and has been shortlisted for the Dermot Healy Poetry Prize and many other awards.

Cory Ingram is emerging Canadian writer interested in exploring issues of climate change, personal identity, and minority/LGBTQ experience through prose, poetry, and graphic design. His debut novel, *Paradise,* was published by Ganymede Press in 2020.

Shirin Jindani has published in *Staple, Envoi* and *RISE* and was highly commended in the 2019 Westport International Poetry Competition.

Breda Joyce lives near Cahir, Co. Tipperary, Ireland. Her first collection *Noctiluca* is to be published by Chaffinch Press Spring 2021.

Julie Kane is a former National Poetry Series winner, Donald Justice Poetry Prize winner, Fulbright Scholar in Creative Writing/American Studies (Poetry), and Louisiana State Poet Laureate with poem in more than fifty anthologies including Best American Poetry 2016, currently teaching in the low-residency poetry MFA program at Western Colorado University.

Sadbh Kellet is an Irish writer whose poetry and prose has appeared in journals such as *Strange Times, Paper Lanterns, Aloe, Boyne Berries,* and *Sonder.*
Anthony Lawrence's poems have appeared in *Poetry, The Rialto, Southward, Ink, Sweat & Tears, Prole* and many others. He teaches Writing Poetry at Griffith University and lives on Moreton Bay, Queensland. He has published sixteen collections of poetry.

Aifric Mac Aodha has published *Gabháil Syrinx* in Irish. She is a recipient of the Oireachtas Prize for Poetry. Gallery Press published a bilingual collection with English translations by David Wheatley *Foreign News* (2017).

Derek Mahon was one of the finest poets ever to write in the English lanuage. He died a month before this book went to press. *Washing Up* (Gallery Press, 2020) has appeared posthumously.

Paul Mariani an American poet and biographer, with nine volumes of poetry published to date as well as six biographies (William Carlos Williams, Hart Crane, Wallace Stevens, John Berryman, Robert Lowell, and Gerard Manley Hopkins) and several books of essays.

John McAuliffe has published five collections with The Gallery Press. His first, *A Better Life* (2002), was shortlisted for a Forward Prize. His second collection *Next Door* was published in 2007, *Of All Places* (a Poetry Book Society Recommendation) in 2011 and *The Way In* (2015). His fifth collection, *The Kabul Olympics*, was published in April 2020.

Thomas McCarthy is a member of Aosdána. He has won the Patrick Kavanagh Award, the Alice Hunt Bartlett Prize and the O'Shaughnessy Prize for Poetry as well as the Ireland Funds Annual Literary Award. He has published ten poetry collections most recently *Prophecy* (Carcanet 2019)

Jon McLeod was born in South Australia but grew up in the North West of England. His poetry has appeared in a number of magazines, including *The North* and his work also featured in a recent anthology of poetry on the theme of running, *The Result is What You See Today.*

Afric McGlinchey is the author of two poetry collections, *The lucky star of hidden things* and *Ghost of the Fisher Cat* (both published by Salmon Poetry and translated into Italian by L'Arcolaio) and a chapbook, *Invisible Insane* (SurVision). Her forthcoming auto-fictional memoir, *Tied to the Wind*, will be published by Broken Sleep Books in 2021.

John Mee won the Patrick Kavanagh Award in 2015. In 2016, he won first prize in the Fool for Poetry International Chapbook Competition. *From the Extinct* was published by Southword Editions in 2017.

Sighle Meehan has been published in *Poetry Ireland Review, The Stinging Fly, Skylight 47, Fish Anthology, Best British and Irish Poets* 2019 (Eyewear), and *Universal Oneness* (New Delhi).

Tyler Mills is the author of *The City Scattered* (winner of the Snowbound Chapbook Award, Tupelo Press 2022), as well as *Hawk Parable* (winner of the Akron Poetry Prize, University of Akron Press 2019) and *Tongue Lyre* (winner of the Crab Orchard Series in Poetry First Book Award, Southern Illinois University Press 2013).

Audrey Molloy is an Irish poet. Her debut collection, *The Important Things*, will be published by The Gallery Press in 2021. Her chapbook, *Satyress*, was published by Southword Editions in 2020.

Kim Moore's prize-winning pamphlet, *If we could speak like wolves* (Smith-Doorstop) was chosen as an Independent Book of the Year in 2012 and was shortlisted for other prizes. Moore won an Eric Gregory Award in 2011 and the Geoffrey Dearmer Prize in 2010. The *Art of Falling* (Seren 2015) is her debut collection.

Jed Myers is author of *Watching the Perseids* (Sacramento Poetry Center Book Award), *The Marriage of Space and Time* (MoonPath Press), and four chapbooks, He lives in Seattle and edits poetry for *Bracken.*

Eiléan Ní Chuilleanáin is a member of Aosdána. She has published eleven collections of poetry with the Gallery Press. Among her honours are the Patrick Kavanagh Prize and the Griffin Poetry Prize.

Mary Noonan has published two poetry collections *The Fado House* (2012) and *Stone Girl* (2019), both with the Dedalus Press. She has received Literature Bursaries from the Arts Council.

Lani O'Hanlon is a movement therapist and the author of *The Little Theatre* (Artlinks, 2017) and *Dancing the Rainbow* (Mercier Press, 2007). She has an MA in creative writing from Lancaster University.

Keith Payne has published a collection *Broken Hill,* (Lapwing Publications) in 2015 and *Six Galician Poets,* (Arc Publications 2016). *Diary of Crosses Green,* from the Galician of Martín Veiga (2019).

Cheryll Pearson's first collection *Oysterlight* was published by the Pindrop Press in 2017. She lives and works in Manchester.

Maya C. Popa 's first full collection *American Faith* was published by Sarabande in 2019. *The Bees Have Been Cancelled* (Southword Editions 2017) was a PBS Pamphlet Choice. She lives in New York

Laura Potts is a writer from West Yorkshire. A recipient of the Foyle Young Poets Award, her work has been published by *Aesthetica, The Moth* and The Poetry Business. She was shortlisted for The Edward Thomas Fellowship in 2020

Greg Rappleye teaches in the English Department at Hope College in Holland, Michigan. He has published four collections of poetry, most recently *Tropical Landscape with Ten Hummingbirds,* (Dos Madres Press 2018).

Nell Regan is a poet and non-fiction writer. Her third collection is *One Still Thing* (Enitharmon Press, London). She has been a Fellow at the International Writers Programme, Iowa and recipient of an Arts Council Literature Bursary. Forthcoming from Dedalus Press is her co-translation from the Japanese of Oguru's *100 Poets: 100 Poems.*

Mara Adamitz Scrupe is a poet and visual artist and the author of six award-winning poetry collections, most recently *in the bare bones house of was* (Brighthorse Press 2020). She lives in the Blue Ridge Mountains of Virginia.

Alan Shapiro has published over ten books of poetry, most recently *Against Translation* (2019). *Reel to Reel* (2014) was a finalist for the Pulizer Prize, *Night of the Republic* (2012) was a finalist for the National Book Award and the Griffin Prize, and *Old War* (2008) won the Ambassador Book Award.

Peter Sirr's most recent collections are *The Gravity Wave* (2019), a Poetry Book Society recommendation and *Sway* (2016), versions of poems from the troubadour tradition. *The Rooms* (2014) was shortlisted for the Irish Times Poetry Now Award and the Pigott Poetry Prize. *The Thing Is* (2009), was awarded the Michael Hartnett Prize in 2011. He is a member of Aosdána.

Gerard Smyth has published ten collections of poetry, most recently *The Sundays of Eternity* (Dedalus Press 2020). He is a member of Aosdána.

Breda Spaight is 2020 winner of the Doolin Poetry Prize. Her debut chapbook *The Untimely Death of My Mother's Hens* is available from Southword Editions.

Rebecca Tamás is the editor, with Sarah Shin, of *Spells: Occult Poetry for the 21st Century*, published by Ignota Books. Her first full length collection of poetry, *WITCH*, (Penned in the Margins 2019) was a Poetry Book Society Spring Recommendation, a Guardian Poetry Choice, and a Paris Review Staff Pick.

Alyssandra Tobin is a poet from the Northeast USA, and has had work published in *Bodega, Hobart, Juked*, and elsewhere. She earned her MA at University College Cork, and is currently an MFA candidate in Poetry at the University of Montana. She reads for *Electric Literature*, and is a poetry editor at *CutBank* literary magazine.

Heather Treseler's poems appear in *PN Review, Harvard Review*, and *Cincinnati Review*, among other journals. *Parturition* (Southword Editions 2020) won the Fool for Poetry Competition and the Jean Pedrick Chapbook Award from the New England Poetry Club. She is Associate Professor of English at Worcester State University.

Brian Turner has published two poetry collections *Here Bullet* (Alice James 2005) and *Phantom Noise* (Alice James/Bloodaxe 2010). He was the inaugural John Montague Poetry Fellow. He lives in Florida. He is Director of the low-residency MFA program at Sierra Nevada College at Lake Tahoe.

Martín Veiga has published six award-winning poetry collections in Galician. *Diary of Crosses Green* translated by Keith Payne appeared in 2018. He lives in Cork where he lectures at UCC.

Anthony Walton is an American poet and writer. His work has appeared widely including *The New Yorker, Kenyon Review, Oxford American*, and *Rainbow Darkness*. He is currently a professor and the writer-in-residence at Bowdoin College in Brunswick, Maine.

David Wheatley has published five collections of poetry, most recently *The President of Planet Earth* (Caracanet 2017). His has published a collection of translations of Aifric Mac Aodha's poems *Foreign News* (Gallery Press 2017)

Enda Wyley was born in Dublin and has published six collections of poetry with Dedalus Press, including *Borrowed Space, New and Selected Poems*. Her recent collection, *The Painter on his Bike*, was published by Dedalus Press, 2019. She is a member of Aosdána.

Printed in Poland
by Amazon Fulfillment
Poland Sp. z o.o., Wrocław

65679603R00083